HORIZON

SPRING, 1971 · VOLUME XIII, NUMBER 2

ᴄHorizon

SPRING, 1971 · VOLUME XIII, NUMBER 2

EDITOR IN CHIEF
Joseph J. Thorndike

EDITOR
Charles L. Mee, Jr.
MANAGING EDITOR: Robert Cowley
ART EDITOR: Jane Wilson
ART DIRECTOR: Kenneth Munowitz
ASSOCIATE EDITORS: Shirley Tomkievicz, Ormonde de Kay, Jr.
CONTRIBUTING EDITORS: Walter Karp, Barbara Klaw
ASSISTANT EDITOR: Mary Sherman Parsons
EDITORIAL ASSISTANTS: W. Jeffrey Simpson, Sue Ferris
COPY EDITOR: Mary Ann Pfeiffer
ASSISTANT COPY EDITOR: Kaethe Ellis

ADVISORY BOARD
Gilbert Highet, *Chairman,* Frederick Burkhardt,
William Harlan Hale, John Walker
EUROPEAN CONSULTING EDITOR: J. H. Plumb, *Christ's College, Cambridge*
CHIEF, EUROPEAN BUREAU, Gertrudis Feliu, *11 rue du Bouloi, Paris 1er*

AMERICAN HERITAGE PUBLISHING COMPANY
PRESIDENT AND PUBLISHER
Paul Gottlieb

EDITORIAL ART DIRECTOR
Murray Belsky

SENIOR EDITORS, HORIZON
Marshall B. Davidson
Oliver Jensen

HORIZON is published every three months by American Heritage Publishing Co., Inc. Editorial and executive offices: 551 Fifth Avenue, New York, N.Y. 10017. Treasurer: Marjorie C. Dyer. Secretary: John C. Taylor 3rd. All correspondence about subscriptions should be addressed to: HORIZON Subscription Office, 379 West Center St., Marion, Ohio 43302.

Single copies: $6.00. Subscriptions: $20.00 per year in the U.S. and Canada; elsewhere, $21.00.

Cumulative indexes for Volumes I–V and VI–X are available at $3. HORIZON is also indexed in the *Readers' Guide to Periodical Literature.* The editors welcome contributions but can assume no responsibility for unsolicited material. Title registered U.S. Patent Office. Second-class postage paid at New York, N.Y., and at additional mailing offices.

Battle of the Sexists

In a celebrated scene from the *Bourgeois Gentilhomme* by Molière, the *gentilhomme,* who has recently taken to the studious life, learns with delight that for the past forty years he has been speaking prose, "without knowing it." As this issue of HORIZON goes to press, the editors perceive with delight that they have given the magazine a central theme, without knowing it: women.

The lead article is, of course, wholly intentional. "The Feminine Utopia" by Walter Karp takes the long view of the Women's Liberation Movement, the latest, angriest manifestation of militant feminism. Women, says Mr. Karp, may do as they please, but once they have children they owe it to the human race, literally, to stay home and take care of them. For the children's sake, therefore, rather than for purposes of sexist oppression, society has assigned to man the role of provider and protector. Mothers belong at home, and perhaps also in community politics—which, God knows, could use some touch of civility.

To many, this argument will look like gussied-up male chauvinism. But Mr. Karp raises a question that is hard to duck. If women are to become the social, sexual, and economic equals of men, the institution of the family—the "nuclear" family, as sociologists fondly call it—must undergo a drastic change. For it is common knowledge that years of patient nurture are required to turn children into civilized adults. Who is to undertake that task? Mother? The Merry Moppets Day-Care Centers, Inc.? Or Big Brother? According to J. H. Plumb, whose article on a new kind of family begins on page 60, the old-fashioned domestic unit is already outmoded, and is already being replaced by more appropriate forms.

But even the most dedicated women's liberationist would surely concede that all the battalions of porcine male chauvinists that history has mustered have not succeeded in enslaving *all* women. Observe the Wife of Bath, a paragon of energetic womanhood, described by Chaucer around 1387 and by Anthony Burgess in his article on *The Canterbury Tales* (see page 44). No poor slave she, who has worn out five husbands! The feminine mystique she embodies is nothing like the one that drives the smoldering housewife on her rounds.

Commonplace and earth-bound as the Wife of Bath may be, she is akin to Astarte, the great mother goddess of the Near East. As Kenneth Cavander's article depicts her, she was "a goddess of life-giving nature, a suprahuman embodiment of the creative forces of the universe." Her image may be hard to rediscover in the modern world. Nevertheless, femininity is, and always has been, something more than a political and economic tool, an excuse for social oppression, a *casus belli*.

Anyone conversant with the history of the world since 1776 knows that predicting the outcome of liberation movements is risky. Women's Lib may actually bring about "a truly androgynous society," as one of its adherents calls it, "in which both sexes will be free to develop and contribute to their full potential"; or it may collaborate in the production of a totalitarian nightmare, as Mr. Karp fears; or its achievements may be less portentous than either of these extremes. Meanwhile, Kate Millett and the sisters have successfully provoked a re-examination of male and female roles in life. *Sexual Politics* is one of those books that permanently affect one's vision. Nothing quite appears the same anymore. Turn, for example, to page 94, and look at Giorgione's *Tempesta*—a most beautiful and mystifying painting, which generations of scholars have labored to explain.

But having pondered sexual equality, what do we see? A human couple—a woman nursing her baby, a man apparently standing guard—and the skies darkening. Yet something is wrong. The woman seems unloving toward her child and oblivious to the man; he stands apart, staring into space. Did Giorgione intend us to speculate on this odd relationship? Or are we perceiving the painting through the cloud of dust raised by the latest clash of the sexes? Whatever the case, our speculation can do the painting no harm. As for Women's Lib, it has caused us to look at history, and ourselves, with new eyes. For that, at least, we are in its debt. —S.T.

K.MUNOWITZ

COVER: A demure Eve presents the fateful apple to an innocent Adam and ushers in the fall of man in a painting by Lucas Cranach the Elder. Today another kind of fall of man is being proposed by the Women's Liberation Movement with its vigorous attack on male domination. The controversial subject is discussed in an article beginning on page 4.
LEE COLLECTION, COURTAULD INSTITUTE GALLERIES, LONDON

The Feminine Utopia

In one man's opinion: "A movement that began by asking for a fair share of dignity and human achievement can today think of no other source of dignity, no other source of achievement, than toiling at a job"

The common features of human life have been with us for an immensely long time. Ever since humankind began to make a human world for his habitation, that world has been shared and divided along sexual lines. To the male half, by and large, has gone the responsibility for supporting and protecting females; to the female half, by and large, has gone the responsibility for nurturing children and for maintaining the households in which children are raised. Although we speak, in exalted moments, of "humanity," we see each other as males and females, as men and women, and not simply as fellow human beings. So enduring are these common features that they have come to seem natural, right, and unalterable, the permanent expression of our deepest human nature.

Today, for the first time, they are being attacked in the awesome name of liberty and justice. They are being shown to be not natural but contrived, not right but oppressive—and certainly not unalterable. This sharp and comprehensive attack is led by a protest movement known as Women's Liberation, the re-emergence after about a forty-year hiatus of what used to be called, more simply, the women's movement. It maintains that the common features of the human world are the basis of an ancient and radical injustice, which must now be swept away: the domination of females by males. It is a bold and comprehensive challenge, for if the movement is right, then much of what has passed for human wisdom is false. We would be forced to admit that humankind has been wrong just where we were most certain we were right: in the way we have ordered our most basic institutions to meet the elementary needs of human life. If, on the other hand, the women's movement is wrong, then we must recover half-forgotten fundamentals, fundamentals that have been obscured, I believe, by all that is modern in modern civilization, in order to understand why it is wrong.

The women's movement has a case, and it is a powerful one. That case begins with the simple acknowledgment of what anthropologists have long since confirmed: the ascendancy of males over females is a universal fact of life in every known human society. Virtually everything that a given society considers to be worthy and prestigious, whether it be the making of laws or of wars, the conduct of politics, religion, or business, or even, as Margaret Mead has observed, the dressing of ceremonial dolls, is almost exclusively in the hands of males. The male is the actor, the creator, the keeper of the cults, the inventor of the taboos. He is concerned with most of what is specifically human in the human world, as opposed to what is merely natural, merely biological, merely concerned with life itself.

The French existentialist Simone de Beauvoir pointed out in her classic study, *The Second Sex*, that it is the males who create the values by which life in any society is justified: "At no time has [the female] ever imposed her own law." Even where men looked with awe upon the reproductive powers of females and worshiped Earth Mothers in their image, it was the men who made the gods, as Sir James Frazer, the pioneer student of pagan religion, observed a century ago. In this male-dominated world, human achievement is so much a male prerogative that we use the word "man" in speaking of humanity. It made perfect sense for Aristotle to say, "we must look upon the female character as a sort of natural deficiency"; for Roman law to put females in the custody of males in recognition of feminine "imbecil-

Cranach's Adam, opposite, contemplating this liberated descendant of Eve, might well scratch his head in bewilderment—much as he did when handed the apple. Adam was painted in 1526, more than four centuries before a photographer captured this rain-splattered embodiment of Women's Liberation.

By WALTER KARP

One man's family is dominated by the proud, smiling papa, around whom wife and children cluster for protection and security. Women's Liberation might declare this image to be distorted and degrading, but in the world of today the American male is still ten feet tall.

ity"; for Hebrew males to greet each day with the prayer, "Blessed be God . . . that he has not made me a woman."

Yet this universal ascendancy of males did not just happen. This is the crucial point. It was made possible by the most fundamental of all mankind's social arrangements: the universal institution of the family, the "patterned arrangement of the two sexes," in Dr. Mead's definition, "in which men play a role in the nurturing of women and children" within a "household shared by man or men and female partners into which men bring food and women prepare it." This sexual division of roles, however, is an unequal one. While females are largely confined to the household sphere, males assume responsibility for most of what takes place outside the home. As Mme de Beauvoir has emphasized, the male role in the family is individual, active, and open; the female role, closed and far less individual. Her body, designed for childbearing, becomes within the family her "womanly" destiny, and to that destiny she is asked to submit.

The family, however, is not a natural or a biological institution. It, too, is a human contrivance, and it invites the question, which the women's movement asks, why has the family division of roles been drawn up the way it has? That women bear the children is a biological fact; that those who bear children must carry the chief burden of tending them is not a biological necessity. It is certainly "convenient," as Dr. Mead has pointed out, but convenience is not necessity. There is even less reason for women to maintain the household simply because they are female. Among the Todas of southern India, where women may have more than one spouse, the men, interestingly enough, consider housekeeping too sacred for women.

To justify the sexual division of the human world, it was long supposed (by males) that women were allotted the household role because of their natural incapacity to do much else. They suffered, in Aristotle's phrase, a "natural deficiency" in the ability to think, to act, and to create. Yet there is no evidence, biological or psychological, of any such inherent incapacity in females (the anthropologist Ashley Montagu has even argued that women are "naturally superior"). If females are physically weaker than men, few human achievements require a great amount of muscular strength.

A justification less tainted with male chauvinism—in the women's movement phrase—has long been based on the presumed inherent temperament of females. According to this view, the female is naturally more passive, more tender, more inward-looking and private—in a word, more "feminine"—than the innately more active and aggressive male. It follows that the family division of roles is simply the reflection of this fixed fact of life. Sigmund Freud even constructed an elaborate theory, based on the female's discovery of her presumed anatomical deficiencies, to explain why females manifest a submissive feminine personality.

This theory has proved the most perishable portion of Freud's work because, as Margaret Mead demonstrated in her 1935 study *Sex and Temperament,* there are no innate female or male temperaments. Studying three New Guinea societies, she discovered that in one, the Arapesh, women did indeed exhibit those temperamental traits of passivity, tenderness, and unaggressiveness that Western society has associated with the innately feminine. On the other hand, so did the men. In a neighboring tribe, the Mundugumor, the males exhibited the traits of egotism, boldness, and aggressiveness that we have long associated with the innately male. So, however, did the women. In the third society, the Tchambuli, the "masculine" traits were exhibited by the women and the "feminine" traits by the men. Dr. Mead drew from this the obvious conclusion: "Standardized personality differences between the sexes are . . . cultural creations to which each generation, male and female, is trained to conform."

It has been argued, more plausibly, that there is a natural link between mothers and their offspring, a maternal instinct or a natural sense of fulfillment in tending children that not only explains but justifies the female role within the family. If such a link exists, however, it can only be described as tenuous. There are societies in which hardly a trace of a maternal instinct appears. In one of the New Guinea tribes Dr. Mead studied, the women looked on their maternal role with unconcealed repugnance, and the rare woman who was motherly toward her children was treated with scorn. More striking yet are the Mbaya, studied by the greatest of modern anthropologists, Claude Lévi-Strauss. They look with such disfavor on motherhood that they employ a partial substitute for sexual reproduction: Mbaya warriors capture young prisoners and adopt them as children.

More telling than these isolated examples, however, is a universal fact: few human societies have considered the link between females and their offspring so natural or so fulfilling that they have neglected to teach females that motherhood is their duty and their destiny. Indeed, the more civilized a society becomes, the more insistent this training is likely to become; for the richer the human world grows in the range of its activities, the greater is the temptation of females to desert the household sphere.

In view of these considerations, many spokesmen for the women's movement conclude that males have deliberately confined females to the domestic sphere in a concerted effort to maintain their dominance. Employing an analogy with racism, many today speak of the present system of human life as "sexism"—"the definition of and discrimination against half the human species by the other half," according to Robin Morgan, editor of a recent collection of women's movement essays called *The Sisterhood is Powerful*. The most rigorous exponent of this view is Kate Millett, who has coined the term "sexual politics" (in a well-known book of that title) to designate the ways in which males contrive to keep females subordinate under what she calls "patriarchal government."

Miss Millett and other spokesmen for the movement are willing to admit that Western civilization—the United States in particular—is a "reformed patriarchal society." In this reformed system men and women are political equals, and have been since the general establishment of female suffrage. Most of the legal liabilities women once suffered—the prohibition against wives owning property, for example—have been repealed (though only within the past decade in France). If their opportunities still remain much more limited than those of men, women have won the right to work at paid jobs other than domestic service, to attend universities, and to establish careers. Yet females, in the view of the women's movement, remain subordinate, because they are still "economically dependent" on males, which is to say, husbands. Miss Millett views the entire "sexist" system as the means by which males prevent females from gaining "independence in

"The universal ascendancy of males did not just happen. It was made possible by the most fundamental of all mankind's social arrangements: the universal institution of the family."

7

The traditional female role in the family, symbolized by the nursing mother above, is today being questioned by Women's Liberation advocates. Mothers, they say, should no longer have to conform to what has been, mistakenly, required of them; they should be free to work, to leave their children to be reared in state-run day-care centers. Some might consider this alternative Orwellian; the French children receiving mass toilet-training below will be teen-agers in 1984.

economic life." As Mme de Beauvoir wrote twenty years earlier in Paris, the extent to which women are dominated is the extent to which they are kept "from assuming a place in productive labor." Only when all women are "raised and trained exactly like men . . . to work under the same conditions and for the same wages," will females ever be liberated.

What looms up as the giant barrier to such liberation is, of course, the primal institution of the family. It is the family that directly secures the economic dependence of women, for within the family the female is supported while she herself labors without pay—a point the women's movement finds particularly telling. It is by means of the family division of roles that females are assigned, in Miss Millett's words, to "menial tasks and compulsory child-care," and thus are prevented from taking their place in the work force. It is by virtue of her training for the family that a female is brought up to be feminine, passive, compliant, and unaggressive, and so rendered unfit for winning independence through work.

The conclusion of the movement's argument is not easily avoided, though more moderate elements flinch from the logic of the case. The liberation of females, *all* females, can only come when the family is abolished as the primary unit of human life, to be supplanted, in the words of Miss Millett, by "collective, professionalized care of the young." With the end of the durable family-centered world, females would no longer have to be trained from birth to exhibit and admire domestic and maternal virtues. Legal distinctions, like that between legitimate and illegitimate children, and moral distinctions, like that between fidelity and adultery, would cease to have any meaning. The bond of marriage would be quite unnecessary and would be replaced by "voluntary associations."

In this familyless world females would enjoy "complete sexual autonomy," and their decision to bear children would become a purely voluntary one. Trained alike, sharing alike in the world's labor, men and women would be equals. Except for their differing roles in procreation, they would for the first time in human history be interchangeable, one with the other, as fellow human beings.

Those women's movement spokesmen who propose this "sexual revolution," as it has been called, do not expect that it lies in the immediate offing. What they do maintain is that this must be the ultimate goal of women in their struggle for liberation. They do not promise, in general, that humankind would be *happier* under this new dispensation. What they do say is that this new dispensation would be just and that only such a dispensation can liberate females from the age-old injustice of male domination.

And yet, something seems wrong, and very seriously wrong. At the base of the long and complicated argument propounded by spokesmen for the women's liberation movement lie two seminal assumptions, which deserve more scrutiny than the movement, to date, has given them. The first is the assumption that the family can be replaced successfully by a modern organization of experts, professionals, and salaried employees. The second is the assumption that human dignity is to be found in the organized wage-earning work force.

G. K. Chesterton put his finger on the first assumption in a short essay he wrote some fifty years ago, called "Marriage and the Modern Mind." What, he asked, did the women's movement of his day think about children? The answer was that they did not think about them at all. They would "imitate Rousseau, who left his baby on the doorstep of the Foundling Hospital." They overlooked the problem of children, Chesterton implied, because they saw children not as a problem but merely as an obstacle. Yet every known human society has made the problem of children its primary concern, and has done so because the problem *is* primary.

The most important thing about children is that we must have them. We must reproduce our kind in sufficient numbers to replace those who die. This is so not because we are animals, who cannot recognize, and will not mourn, the possible extinction of their species. It is so because we are human and have made for ourselves a human world whose essential attribute is its permanence. We die, yet it abides. Without that assurance, human life would be unthinkable. But precisely because we inhabit a human world, not even the birth of children is assured: as the women's movement has emphasized, there is no maternal instinct and no natural fulfillment in bringing children into the world. Just so. However, humankind must find some secure and permanent means to ensure that females submit to motherhood, that they continue to sacrifice a large portion of their individuality, for the sake of the human world's survival.

To date, at least, this has been assured by the family. Because of the personal bonds it establishes, the female is not asked to carry out an abstract duty to the species and to the world. She bears children for the sake of her spouse, or for the sake of her father, or for the sake of her mother's clan, according to the form of the family system. By means of the family, duty to the species becomes duty to known persons, to persons united to females by abiding ties of loyalty and affection. But what of the familyless world outlined by the women's movement? In such a world the sexual training of females would be abolished and bearing children would cease, of necessity, to be a deeply felt personal virtue. Under such conditions reproduction would become a public duty, as it was in the garrison state of Sparta, where women, as well as men, were largely liberated from family ties. The personal voice of the family would be replaced by mass exhortation— the voice of the megaphone—urging females to bear children for the good of the State or the Nation or the People.

Such a prospect can be looked on as merely repugnant, but more is at stake than that. To make child rearing a public duty, and mothers into state charges, it is worth remarking, was seen by the Nazis as a perfect means to extend totalitarian control, which is why they exhorted females to bear children out of wedlock in sunny, luxurious nursing homes. The Nazi effort to "liberate" females from the thralldom of husbands was not done, however, for the sake of liberty. A society compelled to make childbearing a public duty is one that puts into the hands of its leaders a vast potential for tyranny and oppression. The "purely voluntary" choice of bearing children might one day have a very hollow ring.

But children pose another problem that the liberationists have not answered satisfactorily. Humankind is not born human, but must be made so through years of patient and watchful care. Yet making the newborn human and fit for the world is an immense and subtle task. Teaching the newborn to speak, to discipline their spontaneous impulses, and to play their roles in adult life is only part of that task,

"Every known human society has made the problem of children its primary concern, and has done so because the problem *is* primary."

"To work is to be free," says Women's Lib. Would the late commuters homeward bound for Westport on the 7:05 agree? Yet, urban mothers, like those seen below on the Portobello Road in London, might gladly exchange the frustrations of child rearing and the laundromat for those of the workaday world.

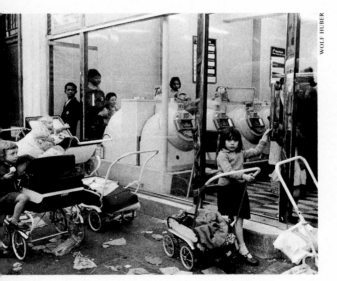

and the most obvious part. In bringing children into the human world, we are bringing them into a moral world and a public world as well. The newborn must learn that modicum of trust in others and that sense of the permanence of things without which humans cannot act together to carry out their purposes. Only a saint need not trust in others or believe in the human world's permanence. In their rearing, too, the newborn must be provided with vivid models of personal loyalty, affection, and respect, or they will never know them at all, never know how to give or how to receive them. They would poison the world in their terrible innocence.

It is the institution of the family that has been assigned the chief role in making the newborn human. This, in truth, is its main purpose. It is the stability of the family, the fact that its members make a permanent home, that gives the newborn that primary sense of the durability and trustworthiness of things on which human action depends. It is because of the personal nature of the family, the fact that it can include within its sphere so many varieties of personal relationships, that the newborn can be endowed at all richly with personal attributes and a human personality.

But again, what of the familyless world of women's liberation? In describing possible family substitutes, spokesmen for the movement have not gone much beyond their cursory remarks about collective and professional child care. The details, however, do not matter as much as the essence of the thing. The care of children would be paid employment; the primary relation of adults to children would be the cash nexus. Child rearing would be an administrative function. That is the heart of the matter.

Certain consequences seem inevitable. From that primary experience of life the young would learn—could not help but learn—that the basic relation of one being to another is the relation of a jobholder to his job. Seeing that the paid functionaries who tended them could be replaced by any other paid functionaries, they would also learn that adults must be looked upon as interchangeable units, individually unique in no important way. Nor is it difficult to imagine the chief virtue the young would acquire should their care be turned into an administrative function. All our experience of bureaucracy tells us what it would be: the virtue of being quick to submit to standardized rules and procedures.

How would the human world appear to a child brought up in such a way? It would appear as a world whose inhabitants are jobholders and nothing more, where there is nothing else for a grownup to be except gainfully employed. What is more, the child would be perfectly raised, by the most basic lessons of his young life, to become another jobholder.

These last considerations touch on a final problem posed for humankind by the fact of birth. In making the newborn human, a way must be found to preserve something of their spontaneity and newness, for if the newness of the newborn is a danger, it is also the spring of hope. A world capable only of duplicating itself in each new generation is a doomed and oppressive one. It is in meeting this problem that the institution of the family exhibits something more than its practicality. It exhibits its one truly irreplaceable virtue, a virtue that lies wholly in its private character.

Because the family is private, it is not quite of the world. It need not share all the world's values, heed all its precepts, or embody all its assumptions. As Dr. Mead has pointed out, it is the peculiar quality of the modern family that no two families are alike. By virtue of its privacy, the family is the primary shelter of human variety. In the very process of preparing its newborn for the world the family can protect them from the world. It can see to it that the world's standards do not impinge too closely upon the defenseless young and so do not mold them too precisely to the world's imperious demands. The young may enter the world without being ignorant of any standard but the world's. In this lies the human potentiality for freedom.

Here the contrast with the collective professionalized care of the young is a stark one. Instead of protecting the young from the world, such administrative child care would fasten the world's ways on the newborn with a strangler's grip. In a society where cash is too often the link between people, it would make cash the sole link between adults and children. In a society where people are being reduced more and more to mere jobholders and paid employees, it would make the child's primary experience of life the experience of being someone's job. In a society showing a remorseless capacity to standardize and depersonalize, it would standardize and depersonalize the world in which children are raised. The ideal world in which females would be liberated for productive labor is a world that would tyrannize the young, which means, in the end, it would tyrannize us all.

Paid labor is freedom and dignity: that is the axiom of the women's movement today. It is not theirs alone. We hear it every day in a hundred different guises. We are told that the dignity of the citizen consists, not in being a free citizen, but in working on a job, that the dignity of the factory worker consists in working in a factory, and that the dignity of the "hard-hat" comes from wearing a hard hat. When an oppressed minority in America demands a citizen's share in power, it is told that what it "really" needs are more and better jobs. That is the common ideology, and if the dream of the women's movement is monstrous, that ideology is its seedbed. The women's movement has simply driven that ideology to its logical conclusion, and the ideal "sexual revolution" is that conclusion.

We must turn, then, to the work world to see what it does offer in the way of human dignity, achievement, and freedom. The first and primary question is that of freedom and its relation to work. The relation is negative. To the Greeks it was axiomatic that those who must labor could not be free. To be free required leisure—even Karl Marx, the philosopher of productive labor, admitted in the end that freedom began when the workday ended. Without leisure, men could not take part in public affairs, could not speak and act in the polis, could not share in power, and thus could not be called free, for those subject to commands are not free. There is nothing abstruse about this, for quite obviously, people work and are paid for their labor even under conditions of abject tyranny and totalitarian domination. In the Soviet Union women play a far more prominent part in the work force than they do in America—most of the doctors in Russia, for example, are women—and thus, by the women's movement definition, are freer than women are here. Yet Russian women enjoy no freedom at all.

The liberationists' blindness to the nature of the work world may have been explained, inadvertently, by Mme de Beauvoir when she pointed out in *The Second Sex* that in comprehending men, women

"The ideal world in which females would be liberated for productive labor is a world that would tyrannize the young, which means, in the end, it would tyrannize us all."

11

CULVER

KEN REGAN—CAMERA 5

*"We are determined to foment a rebellion . . ."
Kate Millett? No, Abigail Adams, writing
to her husband John in March of 1776. She
was content with a mild letter; others have
not acquiesced so readily. The bantamweight
British feminist Emmeline Pankhurst was
carried off to jail in 1906 for her radical
suffragist protests. Her tactics included
hunger strikes, bombs, and arson. Super-
woman today has so far remained a marcher,
like this girl who joined the Women's Lib
demonstration in New York last summer.*

see little more than "the male." So, in looking at the realm of work, the women's movement sees that males, as such, are ascendant. But they have hardly begun to grasp the obvious: that some men are more ascendant than others. When movement spokesmen contrast the "male" role and "male" achievements with the monotonous tasks of the household, many men may well wonder which males they are talking about. According to a statement in *The Sisterhood is Powerful,* "a great many American men are not accustomed to doing monotonous, repetitive work which never ushers in any lasting, let alone important, achievement." It sounds like a typographical error. Most jobs *are* monotonous and do not usher in lasting or important achievements. The majority of jobs are narrow functions, dovetailing with other narrow functions, in large-scale organizations.

Because this is so, most jobs demand few of the moral qualities that mankind has found worthy of admiration. They demand our proficiency, patience, and punctuality, but rarely our courage, loyalty, generosity, and magnanimity, the virtues we mean when we speak of human dignity. The one honorable satisfaction that most men obtain from their labor is the satisfaction of providing for their families, and the women's liberation movement would sacrifice the family for the sake of performing such labors. A movement that began by asking for a fair share of dignity and human achievement can today think of no other source of dignity, no other source of achievement, than toiling at a job. It has looked on the modern mass society, a society in which more and more activities are in the hands of administrations and bureaucracies, a society in which more people are becoming, more and more, merely paid employees, and it has made this mass society its ideal for human life. That, in the end, is the failure of the women's movement.

This failure must be accounted a tragic one—for women *are* kept from their fair share of dignity and achievement; women's talents and moral qualities are too often wasted. A sense of inferiority still clings to the position of women today. The question is, what can be done about it?

The history of the women's movement itself provides, I believe, the basis for an answer. The movement is less than two hundred years old. That some men had power—and women did not—that some men monopolized the privileges and achievements—and women did not— had never before given rise to a movement for female emancipation, or even to any articulate awareness that women were unfree. That awareness did not come until the late eighteenth century, and it came with the rediscovery of political liberty as the Greeks understood it. Not until men asserted their right, as men, to the dignity of the citizen and their right to share in public power was it first borne in upon women that they, as females, were unequal and unfree.

The early leaders of the women's movement grasped this principle firmly. They saw that if men were equal insofar as they were citizens, men and women would be equal when women, too, were citizens. This is why the major struggle of the original women's movement was the fight for the franchise, that necessary condition for political equality between the sexes. The leaders of the movement, women like Susan B. Anthony, saw more in the vote than the simple act of voting. They saw that women would win their dignity—the citizen's dignity—by actively entering public life. They hoped that women by their political activity would help overthrow the political machines that corrupted—and still corrupt—representative government and render the citizenry powerless in all but name. In this they grasped a profound political truth: that men and women would share equally in the dignity and freedom of the citizen only if the republic were truly a republic of self-governing citizens. In a republic where power is monopolized by a few, the very status of "citizen" is empty, and the equality of citizens—male and female—a phantom. In such a corrupted republic women might very well believe that "liberation" is paid labor.

It is often said that the old suffragists were wrong, because enfranchised women did not seize their opportunity. This only proves, however, that the opportunity was wasted. Today, that opportunity lies open as never before. From the point of view of public life women today might even be called privileged. Far more than men, they enjoy the precondition for public life, which is leisure, or at any rate the prerogative of managing their own time. The second advantage they enjoy might be called a sense of locality. While men must shuttle back and forth between their homes and their places of work, it is women who live in local communities, who know what a community is, and it is in local communities that politics begins—at least in the American republic.

The opportunity to enter public life is there, and the will to do so is there as well. There are literally millions of women who thirst for public activity, though they are shunted by the established party machines into mere civic work or stultifying chores in the ranks of party bureaucracies. The old suffragists, however, were talking not of party politics but of nonparty politics, free republican politics that challenged party machines and their monopoly over power. This was—and still is—the crucial point, and there are tens of thousands of communities in which women can make a beginning. When they make that beginning, male ascendancy will near its end, for they would break the hold men still retain over human achievement.

As Susan B. Anthony said a hundred years ago, "they who have the power to make and unmake laws and rulers, are feared and respected." For those women whose gifts and ambitions turn them toward careers in the sphere of work, the public, political activity of women will open doors now shut. Who will be able to say that women are unfit to run a business when they share in that far more demanding activity of governing a community and a nation?

In playing their role as citizens, in helping to restore representative government by their free political activity, women would help restore to men and women alike the freedom and equality of the citizen, "our power and our glory," as Elizabeth Cady Stanton, another pioneer of woman's rights, reminded her audiences a century ago. In helping to do that—and what nobler venture can we undertake?—women would restore to motherhood itself its rightful and proper dignity. That dignity will not come from mass exhortations and mass propaganda, but from the knowledge that freedom bestows upon a free people: the knowledge that it is indeed a grave and noble task to bring up children when we are bringing them up to live in freedom and independence.

This, I believe, is the path that women must take in their struggle for liberation—and because it is a true liberation, it means the enhancement of liberty for all.

"In helping to restore representative government by their free political activity, women would help restore to men and women alike the freedom and equality of the citizen."

One of the few things ever to shock Herodotus, the fifth-century B.C. historian and connoisseur of the exotic, was a custom he came upon in Babylonia. His normally cool manner heats up as he writes:

They have a disgusting practice there. Every woman, at some point in her life, is required to sit in the temple of Aphrodite and sleep with a foreigner. The man pays her a fee and as he does so he is supposed to say, "I hereby invoke the goddess Mylitta."

The "disgusting practice" so repellent to Herodotus had been sanctioned by the Babylonian conqueror Hammurabi more than a thousand years before; it was still in existence nearly a thousand years later, when the Roman emperor Constantine put a stop to it by converting the temples into churches. During all that time, had you visited any large town in the Mediterranean basin or the Near East, you might have witnessed a scene like the following.

Women are arriving at a temple, some on foot, others, not deigning to mix with the mob, in sedan chairs or in carriages. They take up positions in the sacred precinct, wearing a garland of flowers in their hair or a crimson ribbon wound around their waists. There is a constant coming and going of women—young and middle-aged, married and unmarried. Through this crowd wander men, newly arrived from abroad. When one of them points at a woman, or throws some coins into her lap, she gets up and follows him out of the temple. As she goes she jeers at the ones who are left behind; the rule is that no woman may return home until she has performed her sacred duty, and some of the less attractive ones may have to wait years for the chance. Having had intercourse with the man outside the temple, the woman hands over the money to the temple treasury and goes home.

In some temples there are permanent staffs of hierodules, priestesses dedicated to the goddess who prostitute themselves as one of their duties; eventually they, too, hope to be married. So that no one may go away disappointed there are also male prostitutes in attendance.

This temple would have belonged to one of the most powerful and fascinating deities of the ancient world, one whose legend still sets off a sympathetic vibration in the fibers of the twentieth century.

> Woman of women, goddess without equal
> Who guides the destinies of men,
> Noble Queen of the world, sovereign of the sky,
> Lady ruler of the hosts of heaven . . .

A priest-poet of ancient Assyria wrote these lines in honor of Ishtar, the great goddess of his people. The deity he addressed as Ishtar was the same as the Mylitta invoked by the stranger after his anonymous act of love with the woman in the Babylonian temple. Herodotus, translating into Greek, called her Aphrodite. The author of the Biblical Book of Kings fulminates against her as "the abomination Ashtoreth." Her name changed with every change of frontier and tongue, but her nature, seductive and violent, stayed the same. And so let us call her by the name the Phoenicians gave her and carried across the Mediterranean as far west as Carthage—Astarte.

> You are a back door that does not keep out blast and windstorm . . .
> A shoe that pinches the foot of its owner.
> Which love did you love for long? . . .
> Tammuz, the lover of your youth,
> You caused to be mourned year after year. . . .
> You loved Ishullanu, your father's gardener . . .
> Your eyes raised at him, you said:

By KENNETH CAVANDER

The Astarte Phenomenon

Lover and destroyer, bestower of both life and death, this contradictory Near Eastern deity gave herself freely to all men but was "owned" by none. We herewith propose her as the patron goddess of Women's Liberation

IRAQ MUSEUM, BAGHDAD; COURTESY M. E. L. MALLOWAN

In the ancient Assyrian ivory plaque above, Astarte, or one of her votaries, smiles from a window, luring men to serve the goddess through sexual union. The photograph opposite is of a latter-day Astarte, who is seen in a ballet of that name choreographed by Robert Joffrey. It was taken by Herbert Migdoll, whose interpretations of the ballet are included in a portfolio beginning on page 19.

This bronze statuette, found in Palestine (ancient Phoenicia), was made around 2900 B.C. and represents the fertility figure from which Astarte eventually evolved.

"O my Ishullanu, let me taste of your vigor,
Put forth your 'hand' and touch my 'modesty.' "

And Ishullanu said:

". . . Has my mother not baked, have I not eaten,
That I should taste the food of offense and curses? . . ."

Then you struck him down and turned him into a spider. . . .
He cannot go up, nor can he come down.

With these words, Gilgamesh, the hero of the Sumerian epic that survives in truncated, magnificently ornamented verse, reminds the goddess of her many catastrophic love affairs. Tammuz was a beautiful youth—some say her own son. She fell in love with him. Somehow he died, or was killed, and the goddess went down to the underworld in search of him. In her absence "the bull springs not upon the cow, the ass impregnates not the jenny; in the street the man impregnates not the maiden." The world mourns with the goddess. When she reaches the gates of hell, the Queen of Heaven demands to be let in. The goddess cries out to the janitor:

If you do not open the gate
I will smash the door, break the bolt . . .
I will raise up the dead to eat the living
Till the dead outnumber the living.

The janitor opens the gate.

As she passes through, however, Astarte–Ishtar has to give up her crown. By the time she has negotiated the last of the seven gates that separate her from her goal, she is naked. Naked she confronts the Queen of the Dead, who refuses to let Tammuz go and strikes her rival with a disfiguring disease. But the other gods send a rescuer to command the Queen of the Dead to sprinkle Astarte with the waters of life; the Mother Goddess returns safely, recovering her jewels, her garments, and her looks. It is not clear whether she recovers Tammuz as well, but probably a bargain has been struck whereby he stays half the year in the underworld and the other half in the world of light.

With slight variations in detail, the same story appears in myths from Tunis to Babylon, from Norway to the Nile; it is the story of Isis and Osiris, Cybele and Attis, Venus and Adonis, and in its outline it is as simple as the coming and going of the seasons.

But in the dream world of the gods nothing is simple. All features melt and bleed into their opposites. Astarte is the prime example. She is "Woman of Women," "Mother of the World"; the Assyrians addressed her as "Kind Mother," the Phoenicians as "you who prolong life." "Divine Astarte," says a character in a play by the Roman comedian Plautus, "source of strength, life, and health to gods and men." Then, without pause: ". . . and in the same person death, destruction, and carnage." The listener is jolted. How can the goddess who prolongs life be the one to bring it to a violent stop? Nevertheless, it is so.

The temples in which Astarte sat, many-breasted and fecund, were crammed with the spoils of victories she had helped to win. Assyrian generals summoned her aid as they marched into battle; on the island of Cythera she could be seen in her shrine, carved out of wood—and fully armed. She goes one better than the Greek Aphrodite, who only had an affair with Ares; Astarte incorporates Ares and his warlike attributes in her own person. The Mother of Life also wields a sword. Speculating about this contradictory goddess, artists took the contradiction to its ultimate. In some portraits she appears with a beard.

The strain of passionate violence that is woven into the myths about this strange deity is summed up in what must have been one of the most grotesque scenes ever witnessed as part of a divine celebration. Remember that what follows is happening not in some asylum for the insane but in a city long exposed to Greek culture and Roman discipline; the city is Hierapolis, which stood northwest of Aleppo, near the Euphrates, and was a center of religious life for centuries. The description was written by Lucian in the second century after Christ.

Pilgrims arrive in Hierapolis from all over Syria and the neighboring countries. On the days of the festival they crowd into the precinct, and form a circle. In this circle, numbers of people stand around playing flutes, pounding on drums, chanting weird songs from religious texts. Others dance to these sounds, slash their arms till the blood flows, and flagellate each other on the back. At long last, the moment for the creation of the Galli arrives. In the midst of the chanting and flute playing, some of the performers become possessed; even spectators are affected. Suddenly a young man will leap into the center of the circle, rip off his clothes, and snatch up a sword that is ready for him there. Then he severs his genitals and runs through the streets of the town waving them in the air. Choosing a house at random, he hurls them indoors, and whoever lives in that house is required to provide him with woman's clothing and accessories.

And so there was recruited another member of the bands of eunuch priests called Galli, who roamed the ancient Middle East taking up collections for the great mother goddess and putting on mystery plays re-enacting her story. For centuries this and less spectacular cults and rituals associated with Astarte (or whatever name she was called locally) were enormously popular all over the Greco-Roman world.

Then came the conversion of Rome to Christianity, and the temples were closed down, the hierodules sent home, the Galli suppressed. The whole bizarre institution might have remained a skeleton in the closet of the glory that was Greece and the grandeur that was Rome, had not scholars such as Sir James Frazer, along with psychologists and occultists, started to dig into these ancient popular cults and come up with some ingenious, if not always likely, explanations for them.

Some said that temple prostitution was a relic of communal marriage customs, or of the practice found among certain primitive tribes of entrusting the rupture of the hymen to someone other than the husband. Others pointed out that in the ancient world a stranger was looked upon with awe and reverence: might he not be a god in disguise? So the foreigner who impregnated the Babylonian woman was thought to be endowed with magical powers that would ensure her fertility.

Still others saw temple prostitution as a version of human sacrifice, as an extension of the custom of providing sexual hospitality to strangers, as a ritualized form of exogamy. But the theory that gained the greatest support was put forward by Frazer in *The Golden Bough*. Noting that queens and priest-kings sometimes impersonated the goddess and her lover, he said: "The intention of the custom can only have been to ensure the fertility of the land and the increase of cattle and men by means of homeopathetic magic."

All these explanations, including Frazer's, have a rational and pragmatic basis. Are the crops in need of fertilizer? Show them how it's done by doing it yourself. How can the incest taboo be preserved? Keep bringing in strangers. How can you be sure your wife will have babies? Offer her to the first comer in the hope that he is Zeus.

And what about the self-castration of the Galli? Here reason falters.

The Astarte seen in relief on this gold pendant, also from Palestine, holds a lotus blossom in each hand. To the Phoenicians, as to the Egyptians, the lotus was a symbol of the life-giving force—presumably activated by the seductive ways of the goddess.

If the goddess was a temptress and life force, she was also, paradoxically, the embodiment of "death, destruction, and carnage." The stern, armed figure in this stone relief from the eighth century B.C. is Ishtar, as the Assyrians called Astarte. She stands astride a lion, the symbol of violent passions.

Frazer, coming to the end of a steamy passage in Lucian, can only comment wearily, "It is thus that the folly of mankind finds vent in extremes both harmful and deplorable."

What to Frazer was the folly of mankind is to psychoanalysis its bread and butter. Among the psychologists who have dealt with this myth, perhaps the most distinguished is Erich Neumann, a follower of C. G. Jung. Neumann, with Jung, sees in the mythological figures of the Astarte–Aphrodite myth personifications of aspects of the human personality. They are divided by sex—the ego taking the male roles, the unconscious the female. Usually male and female are in conflict, but not always. Sometimes the unconscious helps the ego, even when it (she) appears to be most hostile. Just as a lioness that drives her cubs away from the lair may seem to be cruel but is, in fact, helping her young to survive, so the unconscious that threatens the ego with annihilation may be helping to ensure that ego's survival against the oceanlike flood of the instincts.

The double nature of Astarte, lover and destroyer, would then be an expression of man's feelings about his own irrational instincts and emotions, which threaten to disintegrate his orderly and logical male world but which come irresistibly to tempt and fascinate him in the form of dreams, violent emotions, sexual desire, and uncontrollable fantasies. In the Astarte stories, according to Neumann, ego consciousness is struggling to free itself from this encroaching matriarchal unconsciousness. Rather than succumb to the "Mother," the young lover, who stands for the emerging ego, tries to resist. He flees; he fights; he refuses. But he is not strong enough to win total independence, so he ends up offering what he had tried to withhold—the phallus. Such is the meaning behind the stories of Attis, Narcissus, Hippolytus, and of course, Adonis–Tammuz.

The psychological interpretation has been disputed by many anthropologists and by rival psychologists, but in its emphasis on the subjective character of the *experience* it hits a nerve.

The workings of the male imagination might well produce this distorted cartoon of the female of the species, "more deadly than the male." She lures you and woos you and then, when she has you in her clutches, she breaks you like the giant whom Astarte is said to have reduced to a dwarf. Astarte, in other words, could be a composite portrait of Woman as seen through the nervous and longing eyes of Man—tantalizing, elusive, destructive, but inescapable.

Such an interpretation takes care of the male point of view. But Astarte was first and foremost a goddess of women. To the wives, sisters, mothers, who sat waiting for a stranger to walk up, toss a coin into their laps, take them, and disappear—to these women, who were not especially superstitious or immoral, what did this goddess represent? This is more interesting, perhaps, than what she meant to men.

The epithets and titles that surround Astarte's name must provide a clue to her nature. She is "Silver shining," "Seed producing," "Opener of the womb," "Queen of stars," "Heavenly cow." She is the morning and evening star, the waxing and waning moon. The Queen of the Underworld, sometimes called Allatu, is Astarte's sister, or Astarte herself in another form. Her son-lover, Tammuz, is "The Green One," the world's vegetation, who dies yearly, only to be reborn at the insistence of his mother. Unlike other goddesses of the Near East, she owes her power to no male god-consort; it was she who predicted and

TEXT CONTINUED ON PAGE 27

The many-breasted Diana of Ephesus closely resembled Astarte: she was the primal mother, worshiped in bizarre rituals that involved sacred prostitutes and eunuch priests.

Astarte:

A Portfolio of Photographs by Herbert Migdoll

The color photograph above and those on the following pages—glimpses from the ballet *Astarte,* which Robert Joffrey choreographed and which his company has been performing since 1967 at the City Center in New York—are the work of a young photographer-designer named Herbert Migdoll. They are interpretations of what takes place on stage, montages, built up from layers of color images, that express Migdoll's imaginative conception of this modern re-creation of the ancient myth. The ballet, a multi-media production employing film and accompanied by a hard-rock score, tells of a young man who, fatally drawn to the goddess, struggles fiercely to possess her and finally does so; at the encounter's end, however, she is utterly unaffected. The dancers who appear in these photographs are Trinette Singleton and Nancy Robinson as Astarte and Maximiliano Zomosa, Dermot Burke, and Christian Holder as the young man.

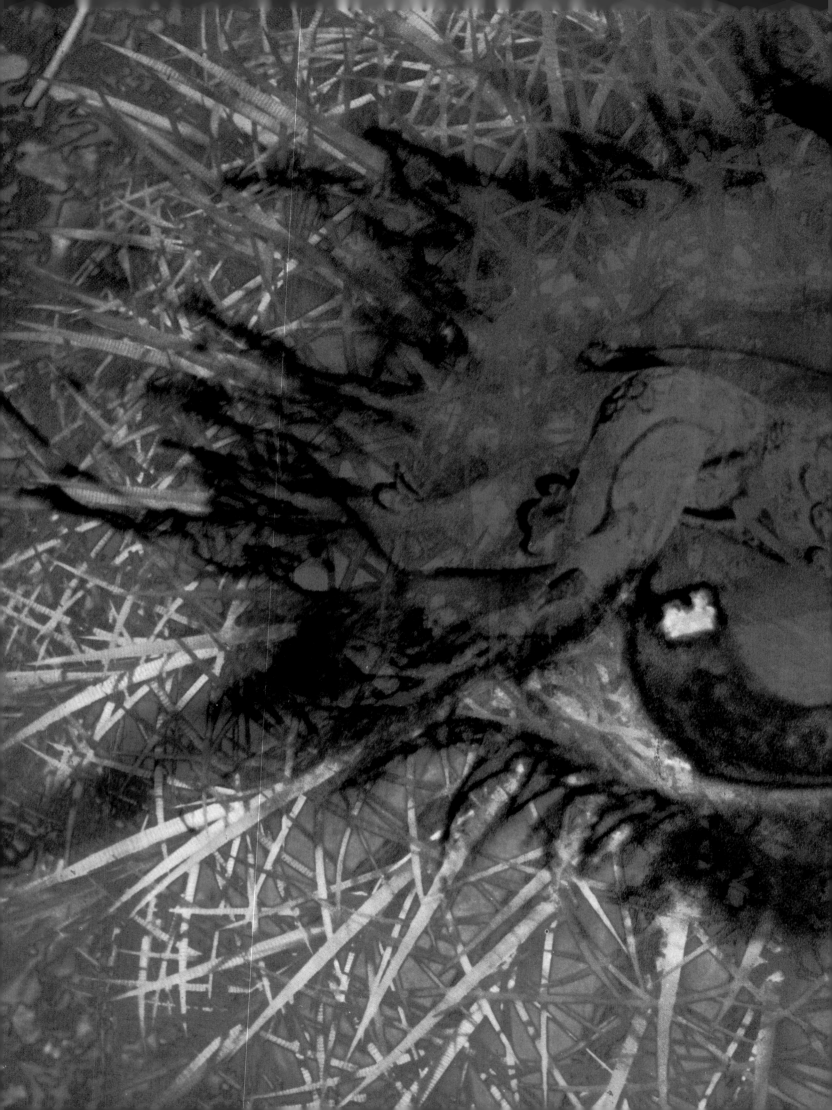

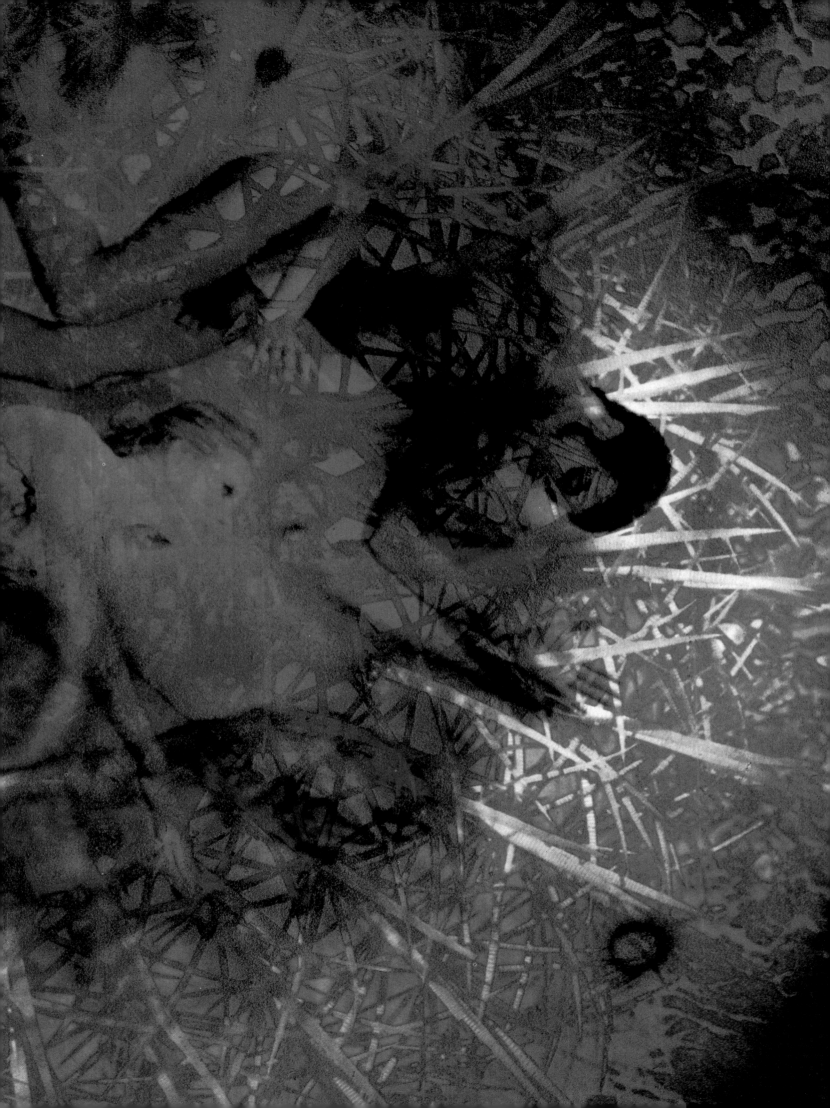

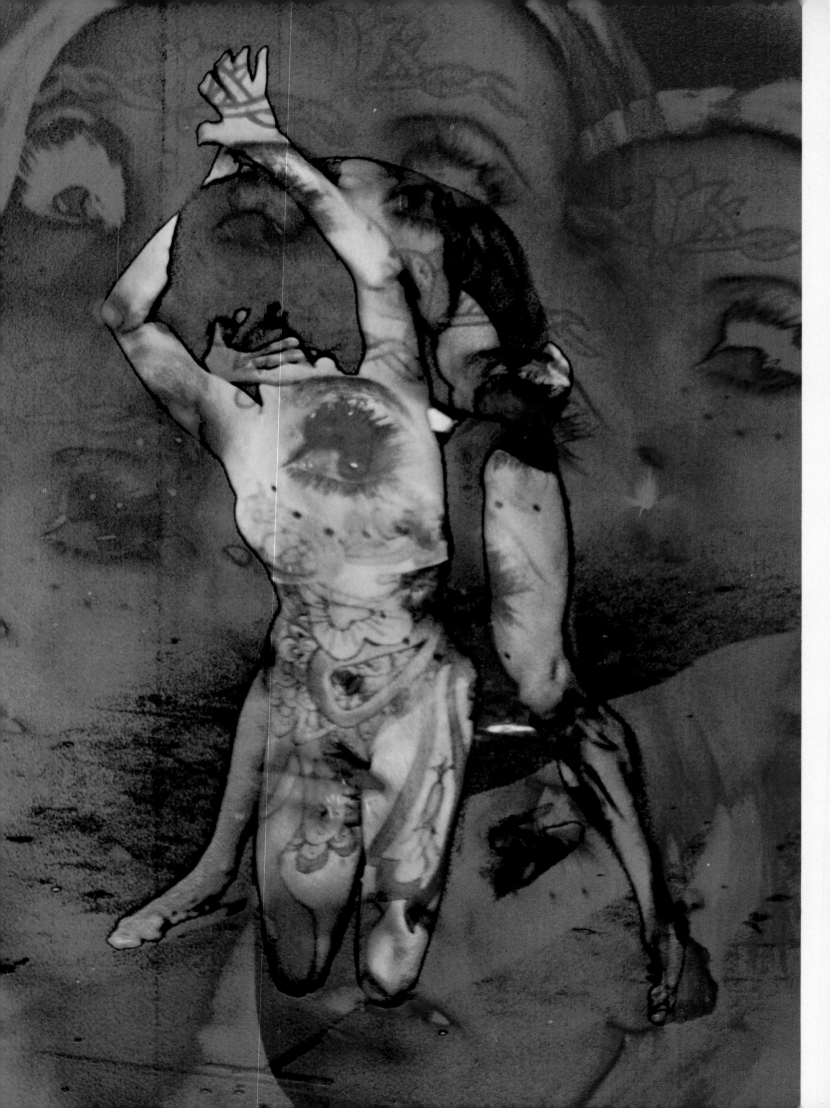

TEXT CONTINUED FROM PAGE 18

brought about the great flood of Babylonian mythology and then came out in a moon boat, an ark, to save man and beast. In short, she is a goddess of life-giving nature, a suprahuman embodiment of the creative forces of the universe.

But she is not identical with these forces. She has a human form and is given human emotions, which can be used for both good and ill. In the individual woman Astarte's powers may manifest themselves as sexual attraction used cold-bloodedly to prove the woman's power, or as a means of gaining a husband and a home, or as the maternal love that is really a way for the woman to fulfill herself through her child.

But when a woman sat in the temple of Astarte, she did so impersonally, not in order to prove her sexual power over men. The man she slept with was not chosen by her. And at the end of the act of sex he was forgotten and his money went to the goddess. The woman got no selfish, or egotistical, reward. On the contrary, she seemed to be acknowledging a principle of love independent of any particular man or material gain such as matrimony or children. The specifically human emotions, embodied in Astarte, were therefore raised to a higher level, given a religious significance, and transformed.

There is a sonnet of John Donne's that ends with the lines:

> . . . for I,
> Except you enthrall me, never shall be free
> Nor ever chaste except you ravish me.

The same concept appears in the worship of the great goddess, who stays chaste in spite of all her lovers. She is virgin, which is not a biological state, but means "free," "unconditioned," "subject to no man." She is Queen of Heaven, and her power stems from no male consort among the gods. An eighth-century Sufi woman mystic, Rabiah, expressed the idea in language strikingly similar to Donne's:

> I have made Thee (God), the Companion of my heart.
> But my body is available for those who desire its company.
> My body is friendly towards its guests.
> But the Beloved of my heart is the Guest of my soul.

Looked at in this way, the son who dies and is then reborn becomes an image for the other great sacrifice a woman must make—that of her children, whom she must give up and let go into the world. Sometimes this appears as a sacrifice of a part of herself, and the mother tells herself that it is only her great love for her child that prevents her from making it. But in fact the love for her child can be a masquerade for a selfish love that stands in the way of both of them.

The Astarte myth may have many meanings—a different one for each age, personality type, or individual. For us, it might become the passion play of the newly awakened Women's Liberation Movement. The Babylonian woman observed by Herodotus belonged to the first man who came along, but in reality she "belonged" to no man. Like her modern counterpart, she wished to be subject no more to the male, with his exclusively masculine standards and values: she existed in and for herself alone, like Astarte. In identifying with the great goddess—virgin and mother, lover and destroyer—she was, if you like, liberated.

Born in Prague and educated in England, Kenneth Cavander now lives in Connecticut. A free-lance writer on the theatre and other performing arts, he is a former teacher of classics and mythology at Yale University.

LOUVRE—GIRAUDON

It comes, perhaps, as something of a shock to realize that the bland and almost-too-familiar Venus de Milo is, in fact, a late representation of the rapacious love goddess Astarte. The Greeks and Romans adopted her as Aphrodite and Venus respectively, but transferred her warlike characteristcs to other divinities, most of whom were male.

MAN
THE HUNTER

Five million years ago a small band of
hominids called australopithecines abandoned a vegetarian diet
in favor of meat. From them, man the hunter
evolved—with all his predatory instincts, his distrust of strangers,
and his notions of family and friends

BRITISH MUSEUM (NATURAL HISTORY)

In this reconstruction, our first hunting ancestor, the australopithecine, chases game on the African plains.

Whatever one happens to think about the future of man, and the pessimists seem more vocal than the optimists nowadays, we have certainly enjoyed a spectacular past. Indeed, viewed in broad biological perspective, the past has been a success story without precedent. The first "hominid," the first member of the family of man, started out as nobody in particular, as a face in the crowd. He was one species among a wide variety of primates, and not a particularly distinguished species at that. Most of his fellow primates had been around a long time before he arrived on the scene and were more fully adapted to life in the trees.

That was some fifteen to twenty million years ago, only yesterday in evolutionary terms, and a great deal has happened since then. A near ape confined to narrow stretches in and around tropical forests has developed into the most widespread of all primates. We live practically anywhere—in treeless polar regions, in bare and bone-dry desert places, in the thin atmosphere of mountain slopes more than three miles high—and our eyes are currently on the stars, on the possibility of settling elsewhere in the solar system or beyond. We, the descendants of a minor breed, have become dominant with a vengeance, the only species with the power to remake or ruin a planet.

There can be no simple explanation for the phenomenon of man. But considerable evidence supports the notion that one of the major forces in prehistory, in the process that led to human beings, was the rise of hunting. Hunting represented a significant break with deep-rooted primate traditions. All primates but man live predominantly on plant foods, and if our ancestors had followed established feeding patterns and remained vegetarians, the odds are that we would still be more apish than human, still be wild animals foraging in the wilderness.

Hunting was no exception to the general rule that far-reaching changes in human evolution—in the evolution of all species, for that matter—come

at a slow pace rather than in melodramatic bursts. In the beginning it was simply a case of stopgap measures calculated to obtain a somewhat larger supply of food than could be provided by plants alone, an activity that apparently could be pursued without radical changes in living habits. But there were changes as hunting became more and more prevalent, until it resulted in the reshaping of hominids both biologically and socially, and to such an extent that important aspects of our behavior today reflect the persisting influence of events that took place during the distant prehistoric past.

According to continuing research, much of it not yet published, this development included the three following stages:

Individual hunting. A stage during which hominids went chiefly after small game and probably did some scavenging; starting perhaps 5,000,000 or more years ago.

Group hunting. This stage was marked by an increasing emphasis on big game, sharing, and sexual division of labor, and began about 1,500,000 years ago.

Corporate hunting. The final stage probably featured the exploitation of great migratory herds on a large-scale, systematic basis, with long-range planning and food storage, and started some 40,000 to 50,000 years ago.

For a glimpse of the earliest hunting hominids, imagine that you are a spectator transported by a time machine to a world long since vanished, an African savanna world that still belongs to zebras and giraffes and vast antelope herds and their predators. Some strange and yet half-familiar animals are squatting not far from a rocky ledge, feeding on grass and roots. They look rather like small chimpanzees, except that when one of them hears a rustling sound, he stands upright like a man and listens intently, with a surprisingly human expression on his face.

Suddenly he sees what made the noise, a hare moving near a low thornbush, and is off after it. The chase ends

quickly. The hare darts away in a swift zigzag path, easily outdistancing its pursuer for fifty yards or so, and seems well on its way toward a successful escape. But then it leaps over a log and freezes in its tracks on the other side, crouching against the ground as though being stone-still would make it invisible. The hominid comes running up to the log, reaches over to grab the hare, and kills it with one neck-wringing motion. Picking up a sharp rock, he proceeds to dismember his victim and eat it raw on the spot.

This brief and hypothetical encounter is based partly on studies of fossil remains found in Africa during the past forty-five years and partly on observations of the behavior of living primates in the wild. The first hunters weighed fifty pounds or so on the average, stood about four feet tall, and belonged to a breed known as "australopithecines," or "southern apes," although the name does not do them justice. They were rather less than humans, to be sure, but considerably more than apes.

The australopithecines were a product of ten million years of evolution. Their predecessors had begun shifting from fruits and other forest foods to such open-savanna fare as grasses and roots and grains, perhaps because of population pressure in the trees, and not long before, the australopithecines had lived on a similar diet. Now they were vegetarians in the process of being corrupted. Not that meat eating is remarkable for primates. Contemporary savanna-dwelling baboons will eat vervet monkeys, hares, and fauns that happen to lie in their paths, but only occasionally, and more than 99 per cent of their food is plant food.

But baboons eat larger quantities of meat during droughts, and the australopithecines may have had to do the same. For them, however, it was not a matter of occasional dry-season emergencies. Dry conditions were spreading over wide continental areas, producing a permanent "emergency," which is probably the chief factor that brought about meat eating on a regular basis.

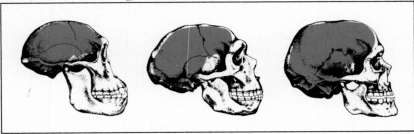

The skulls and brains of the australopithecine, Neanderthal man, and Cro-Magnon man are shown left to right. A big-game hunter, Neanderthal man had a human-sized brain, but lacked the cerebral development of the fully human Cro-Magnon man.

The practice started at least two or three million years ago, the age of the oldest known stone tools (bashing and cutting tools found during the past year near Lake Rudolf in Kenya), and may well have started two to three million years before that.

We can make some educated guesses about the hunting techniques of remote prehistory. For example, like the aborigines of the Australian Western Desert, our ancestors may have erected blinds near water holes, piles of rocks behind which they could hide until their prey came within striking distance. They were probably capable of building such simple structures. Excavating in the Olduvai Gorge—one of the world's richest sites for hominid remains—Louis Leakey, director of the Center for Prehistory and Paleontology in Nairobi, has found traces of a stone wall or windbreak in deposits nearly two million years old.

Then as now, survival required an intimate knowledge of the ways of other animals, particularly an ability to take advantage of their instincts, their built-in escape tactics. The sight of a potential meal moving away at top speed can be a highly discouraging experience for a relatively sluggish predator, and it takes a special kind of wisdom to keep up the chase, confident that sooner or later the prey will go into a freeze-and-crouch pattern. Hares do this, as do certain birds, including a type of partridge whose bones have been found at some of the oldest Olduvai campsites.

Stalking is another ancient and effective technique. But as Leakey has

learned from years of practice, it demands a measure of patience rarely found among hunters who are not playing for keeps, whose lives do not depend on hunting. Once, near a lake outside Nairobi, he camouflaged himself with leafy branches stuck in his belt and started stalking a gazelle about 250 yards away. He advanced slowly as long as the gazelle had its head down to graze. But whenever it stopped grazing and raised its head to look around, he stopped too. He was always one move ahead of the animal. For example, he anticipated the instant of head-raising: "Just before the gazelle looks up, it seems to raise one shoulder a bit higher than the other. That's my signal to stop moving."

Leakey kept on the alert, observing the positions of other gazelles and nearby birds that might call out in alarm at a sudden movement and give him away. He noted possible sources of food in case his prey should escape, such things as a large snail, birds' nests, and an anthill. At last, after two long hours of stalking, he found himself poised only six feet from the gazelle. The hunt ended when he brought it down with a flying tackle, perfected during his university rugby days.

Hunting resulted in a breakdown, or rather, a partial breakdown, of rugged individualism. As far as getting food is concerned, each member of a troop of nonhuman primates is strictly on its own. That even includes infants after their first year: if a mother is feeding and her infant reaches for some of her food, she will push the child away. But

hunting involves sharing, apparently from the very beginning. The existence of australopithecine base camps suggests that they established places where they could await the return of hunters with meat for the troop.

Inevitably, as the hunters became more ambitious, there was more to share. Small game predominated at the oldest Olduvai living sites—hares, tortoises, rats, lizards, and migratory birds, as well as the young of various antelopes. But excavations at later sites in Africa and Europe indicate a gradually increasing preference for a diet that included a higher proportion of big game, a change dictated largely by economics. It may take many hours of intensive small-game hunting to yield the amount of food represented by the killing of a single large antelope. Two or three men hunting together for big game in abundant savanna lands can obtain far more than two or three times as much meat as a lone man in search of small game.

Such tactics were important not only as a way of obtaining meat in large packages. From the standpoint of survival, they were not strictly necessary. Our prehistoric ancestors could, and often did, get along quite adequately, if less efficiently, on a diet consisting solely of small game and various kinds of plants. The shift to the hunting of big game is noteworthy mainly for its social impact. In fact, it helped trigger the most significant chain of developments in the evolution of hominids since they came down from the trees and took up meat eating in the first place.

This trend probably began gathering momentum between 2,000,000 and 1,000,000 B.C., and was certainly well established by about 300,000 years ago. The oldest known prehistoric site outside Africa, the Vallonet cave located on a Mediterranean cliff in France, contains a few chopping tools that were used nearly a million years ago and a museumful of large-animal fossils, including those of rhinoceros, hippopotamus, brown bear, wild boar, and deer. A somewhat more recent site near the village of Torralba in north-central Spain, excavated by Leslie Freeman and Clark Howell of the University of Chicago, has yielded, among other things, the remains of some forty horses and as many elephants, most of which seem to have been deliberately driven into a swamp.

The fossil record hints at the full evolutionary impact of this sort of activity. The period that saw the rise of big-game hunting also saw a notable expansion, and probably a basic reorganization, of the hominid brain and the coming of creatures who had definitely crossed the borderline region between pre-man and man. The most advanced australopithecines had brains with a volume of some 600 cubic centimeters, about the size of a small grapefruit. Estimates based on a study by David Pilbeam of Yale University suggest that within a million years their descendants had brains averaging more than half again as large—and in some cases twice as large, which is almost comparable to the brains of people today.

Pilbeam and other investigators point to a direct relationship between big-game hunting, the development of more complex brains, and the appearance of the first men, members of the species Homo erectus. Natural selection went to work on the hunters. Bands that happened to include individuals with larger-than-average brains tended to outhunt and outlive bands made up of smaller-brained individuals. The inference is that the former were better able to think things through beforehand—preparing ambushes and pitfalls, arranging schedules and signals, using and improving whatever crude form of language they had at the time, and making better tools, a development that seems somehow to have been closely connected with the development of language.

Another advance contributing to the hunting way of life was the use of fire, the earliest known traces of which have been found in a cave not far from Vallonet. The lights went on about 750,000 years ago. Little spots of fire appeared in valleys that had always been dark at night. Fire, originally brought into caves for warmth, acquired another function, that of keeping animals away; and later it was used as an offensive weapon to stampede animals. Signs of burned grass indicate that fire may have been used at Torralba to drive big game into bogs.

Fire also brought a longer day. Hominids, like most forest and savanna animals, had always lived sunrise-to-sunset lives. Now they had extra time to gather at firesides when the hunt was done and review the day's successes and the day's failures, the big ones that got away. The hearth became the first family circle. We have no archaeological proof of ritual activities during this period, but it is quite possible that legends and hunting ceremonies, accompanied by dancing and rhythmical noisemaking, originated around early hearths. Flame and the crackling of burning wood and the moving shadows on cave walls aroused a variety of emotions, and may have served as a kind of stimulant.

Life was becoming more and more complicated, even in those days. The expansion of the brain itself, the most human thing about human beings, introduced a host of difficulties and confronted nature with a bio-engineering problem that has never been solved to everyone's satisfaction. The birth of bigger-brained babies called for an enlarged female pelvic opening and wider hips. But there are limits in that direction, one of them being the fact that wider hips result in an undesirable decrease in running speed and general mobility. So evolution achieved a compromise: hips became a little wider, while babies were born with brains designed to do most of their growing after birth.

The compromise was in line with an established trend in primate evolution; the repercussions have been enormous. The brain of a newborn rhesus monkey has already attained 75 per cent of its final adult size, and the infant is ready to forage for itself at the age of one. But Homo erectus infants came into the world with brains only about a fourth of adult size; the infants were helpless for four or five years, and more completely helpless than the offspring of any other primate. Incapable of either following or clinging to their mothers, they evolved special ways of actively attracting and summoning grownups, notably with the smile and an entire repertory of cries.

Bigger brains affected the habits of mothers as well as those of infants. Prolonged infant dependency meant prolonged maternal dependency. Just as infants needed a mother's care longer, so mothers relied more than ever before on males for defense, help in obtaining food and firewood, and more active participation in the rearing of offspring. The psychoanalyst Erik Erikson of Harvard speaks of the fear of being abandoned as "the most basic feminine fear, extending over the whole of a woman's existence," and that fear may have developed during Homo erectus times, along with new ways of attracting and holding males.

The typical pattern for female primates, for all female mammals, is to be sexually receptive during a brief period of the month only. They come into estrus, or sexual heat, at or immediately following ovulation, tending to be indifferent and unreceptive during the rest of the month. The human female is the only female in which estrus has disappeared, and according to one theory, the evolutionary advantage of the disappearance was that she could become sexually receptive throughout the month and thus improve her chances of tying the male, and eventually a particular male, more securely to her and her offspring.

Developments like these marked the beginnings of monogamy, and an early phase in the prehistory of the human sort of love. They also marked changes in males, changes emphasized in an important study by Lionel Tiger of Rutgers University. Male-male ties were becoming stronger, along with male-female ties. Hunting gave a new meaning to the feelings of man for man. Relationships became closer, more emotionally charged, in the excitement of the chase and the kill, the satisfaction of working as a team, and the sharing of intense experiences and nights at remote camps.

Larger brains, prolonged infant and maternal dependency, changes in sexual behavior—these were some of the consequences of the new kind of primate co-operation that came when a few men began making a regular practice of going out together to kill meat on the hoof. But the story of hunting has another, a final, chapter. The shaping of modern man may have been related to further advances in the technology of killing big game and may have involved events following the appearance of Neanderthal man about 100,000 years ago.

Neanderthal man was a full-fledged member of our species, Homo sapiens, which had appeared more than 150 millenniums earlier with the passing of Homo erectus. His forehead was lower and more sloping than ours, and he had heavier limbs and heavy bone ridges over his eyes. Contrary to popular opinion, however, he was neither brute nor savage; he stood fully erect and is known to have been a highly accomplished hunter. Investigators who have spent time among the Eskimos still do not understand how he managed to live through the long and bitter glacial winters of western Europe.

His fate was determined not by climate but by the evolution of a superior breed. Neanderthal man represented a special kind of Homo sapiens, a subspecies that never made it, but came very close. He lived always on the verge of becoming fully human, or at least as human as we are. For example, judging by a few recent finds of shapes scratched on bone, he was groping to express something and had a vague feeling for pattern and design.

One region of special interest in the study of Neanderthal man lies at the eastern end of the Mediterranean, along the slopes of mountain ranges running roughly parallel to the coastline of Israel, Syria, and Lebanon. This region includes three sites on which traces of a transitional people have been found, people who were definitely Neanderthals, but not like those typical of western Europe. In a cave and nearby rock shelter on the slopes of Mount Carmel, for example, investigators have excavated the remains of individuals with less massive brow ridges, somewhat more rounded skulls, more prominent chins, and smaller faces. The remains date back 40,000 to 50,000 years.

Sally Binford of the University of New Mexico, an archaeologist who has excavated in the Near East, has a theory about why the change occurred in that region and at that time. For one thing, the climate was becoming slightly drier, producing a pattern of seasonal rainfall and affecting the behavior of wild cattle and other herd animals. During the summer the animals grazed on the relatively damp coastal plains, and during the fall, when grasses became scarce, they moved up along green wooded valleys into the foothills, where highland meadows were watered by late fall rains.

Up to this point in human evolution most hunters probably killed one animal at a time, the idea being to stalk a herd and go after a particular individual, often an individual weakened by advanced age or injury. Lions, wild dogs, and other carnivores use similar tactics, which are well suited for groups of three or four hunters. But conditions were ripe for a change along the slopes of the Near Eastern mountains, and according to Miss Binford, late Neanderthal people had the wits to take advantage of their opportunities.

This was the beginning of corporate hunting, with its emphasis, as it were, on "mass production" methods. Large groups of hunters, perhaps as many as twenty to thirty, gathered to wait, not at places where the game was, but at places where their prey could be expected to come in the near future—at narrow passes and natural blinds along the traditional routes of migratory herds. Certain sites in the area are located at such points and include what may be interpreted as further evidence for the Binford theory, a sharp increase in the proportion of wild-cattle bones. Incidentally, the animals did not behave like the docile, mild-eyed creatures of contemporary pastures; the bulls measured more than six feet at the shoulder and were probably fierce, fast on their feet, and well built for fighting back.

Corporate hunting, the most advanced stage of prehistoric food gathering, may have provided the main stimulus for the coming of the most advanced of the hominids. New tactics presumably brought a new need for the ability to look ahead and devise increasingly sophisticated plans. Great quantities of tools would have to be manufactured beforehand, and individuals assigned to special tasks in preparing ambushes and killing, in large-scale butchering, and finally in sharing the meat. These and other organized activities would have favored the development of the brain, not so much in its over-all size, since Neanderthal man had a brain as large as ours, but in certain areas—especially those areas located at the front and sides of the brain and concerned with language and long-range planning.

The record is clear on one basic point. About 35,000 to 40,000 years ago the heavy-browed Neanderthal man of western Europe was replaced by Cro-Magnon man, and prehistory's golden age had begun, an age that culminated in the magnificent cave art of southern France and Spain. The general opinion is that the newcomers originated in the Near East and adjacent areas, and that they were people essentially like us. Or, to put it another way, we have a great deal in common with them psychologically and socially, which is perhaps the most important reason for the current interest in human evolution among scientists and laymen alike.

The past is not something over and done with. It is alive in man, in the sense that some of the things he does most easily, the things that come most naturally, are hang-over responses considerably less useful and relevant today than they once were. We have been wild animals roaming the wilderness for more than 15,000,-000 years, hunters for perhaps 5,000,000 years, and civilized —or rather, partially and intermittently civilized—for the last few millenniums only. So it is hardly surprising that upon occasion we behave inappropriately.

According to one estimate, the world's total hominid population two or three million years ago was about 125,000 individuals, all of them in Africa. Man has been a minority species so long that he reacts to "ghost" circumstances, circumstances that no longer exist, like the punch-drunk exprize fighter who the instant he hears a bell is up and on his feet in fighting stance. The sight of a stranger in a small town may arouse the precise feelings of hostility and distrust that the sight of a stranger aroused long, long ago, when hominids spent their entire lives as members of small hunting bands and anything new was a shock and a threat.

Being frightened by novelty is only part of man's instinctive small-band psychology, only one sign that he lives partly in a vanished world. His capacity to care for others tends to be limited. Generally speaking, a person feels deep love for a few close relatives only, and perhaps for a few close friends. Beyond that, there is a rather rapid falling off of concern; he is not really moved by the problems and frustra-

PAINTING BY Z. BURIAN, COURTESY OF PAUL HAMLYN LTD.

Neanderthalers drive ibexes over a cliff, exemplifying the most advanced stage of hunting: highly organized mass roundups of game.

tions of people across the street or across the hall. This is fundamentally a hunter's behavior, the psychology of one who lives his life among a few of his fellows, rarely seeing anyone else.

Man's instinct is to take, and to take right now while the taking is good. After ages of living on his own among more numerous species, hunting and being hunted, learning to get his share of food and shelter, he has become a master exploiter. Now he has made a world that no longer has a place for exploiters, and yet his relationship to the land and to other animals continues to be primarily one of exploitation. He continues to behave as though the world were still a place of savannas and virgin forests that covered continents.

The existence of such instincts does not mean that man is doomed, that he is innately a killer and must sooner or later wipe himself out. Of all species Homo sapiens is by far the most adaptable. But change is never easy, and it

demands a real effort—an act of creation—to control and modify behavior rooted in the past. The problem is to design environments as appropriate for modern man as the wilderness was for prehistoric man.

Studies of contemporary hunters, like the Bushmen of Africa's Kalahari Desert, indicate that man has lost certain important things in the process of becoming civilized. In most hunting societies men and women live on equal terms with one another, and murder and warfare are extremely rare. Class distinctions and mass killing come with the passing of the hunt. Furthermore, hunters generally have an easy life. Travelers from affluent societies are responsible for the myth that primitive peoples are, and have always been, engaged in a bitter struggle for survival. Richard Lee of Rutgers reports that the Bushmen require no more than two or three days to obtain a week's supply of food, even in a semi-desert environment. They spend the rest of the time talking, playing games, and visiting friends and relatives. Man has never known true leisure since the end of his hunting days.

These facts do not call for a return to the hunt, a "return to nature." But they provide insights into current efforts to recover the desirable features of a past way of life, equality and nonviolence and leisure, as well as to modify the undesirable features, such as the distrust of strangers and novelty in general. Man today is what he has always been, a creature in transition— and, despite the pessimists, a creature with a future.

John Pfeiffer writes on a wide range of scientific topics and most recently has concentrated on the areas of archaeology and anthropology. His book The Emergence of Man *was published in 1970.*

Portrait of the revolutionary as a young man: this mug shot of Leon Trotsky, taken after his first arrest, comes from the files of the czarist police.

The Rise and Fall and Rise of

Leon Trotsky

When a Stalinist secret agent drove a pickaxe through his brain, his theories of Communism seemed consigned, like him, to the dustbin of history. But Trotsky is back, inspiring a new generation of Marxists and being echoed, reluctantly, by an older one

"Of late," declares a recent British anthology of contemporary revolutionary thought, "a spectre has begun to haunt the Communist parties in Europe: Leon Trotsky. The [pickaxe] that killed Trotsky did not succeed in killing his ideas, and a revival of the theories advocated by Stalin's most powerful and consistent opponent is now seen by many as a Marxist alternative to Stalinism."

At first glance, neither the theme nor the rhetoric seems particularly original. Ever since the exiled Bolshevik leader's assassination in 1940, his loyal disciples—the handful that remained—have been predicting the relatively imminent triumph of their martyred prophet's revolutionary doctrines, and paraphrases of the *Communist Manifesto*'s famous opening sentence crop up periodically in Trotskyist literature. But in an abstract and purely ideological sense the Trotskyist mystique of "Victory in Defeat"—the title of Isaac Deutscher's closing chapter in his classic three-volume biography of Trotsky—has long had some rational foundation.

As Deutscher himself remarks, a certain substratum of Trotskyism, if rarely the same kind of Trotskyism, can be found in the policies, teaching, or revolutionary leadership of Khrushchev, Mao, Tito, Castro, and other prominent Communists of the post-Stalin era. Mao and Castro, for example, both preach the doctrine of ceaseless revolutionary struggle against capitalism and imperialism on a worldwide basis that underlies Trotsky's theory of the Permanent Revolution—the very cornerstone of Trotskyism—though both deviate from Trotsky's classic Marxist internationalism in their preoccupation with the industrially underdeveloped areas of the world. Conversely, while it is hard to detect much Trotskyism in Khrushchev's stress on peaceful coexistence between the capitalist and Communist nations or in the nationalist-bourgeois tendencies of Tito's Yugoslavia, all the "revisionist" Communist leaders have echoed Trotsky's theme of the Revolution Betrayed—another basic Trotskyist dogma—in their criticism of Stalinist despotism.

Trotsky wrote with equal fire and conviction as an apostle of revolution and as the critic of a revolution gone wrong, as a champion of the dictatorship of the proletariat and as the censor of a totalitarian bureaucracy established in its name. It is natural that every variety of Marxist revolutionary, and some who are more revolutionary than Marxist, have found inspiration in his voluminous, often contradictory, writings.

The really new development is the resurgence of Trotskyism as an actual revolutionary movement, with considerable and growing support among the young. Though still a minority within the revolutionary minority, the Trotskyists count in their ranks a number of the most brilliant and dynamic leaders of the New Left. For example, the editor of the British anthology just mentioned, and the author of the passage cited, is a fiery young student agitator named Tariq Ali. The scion of a wealthy and aristocratic Pakistani family, Ali is a Trotskyist militant and the editor of an influential underground publication, *The Black Dwarf.*

Another young European revolutionary representative of the new trend —which seems to worry official Communist leadership in Europe even more than it does the defenders of bourgeois law and order—is Alain Krivine. As the outstanding leader of the Trotskyist Jeunesse Communiste Révolutionnaire, he played a key role in the French student revolt of May, 1968. In the French presidential elections the following year, Krivine, then doing his military service, ran as the candidate of the Communist League, a new Trotskyist organization, and though he was careful to explain that his candidacy was merely a kind of revolutionary put-on to bedevil the bourgeois establishment, he rolled up more than 236,000 votes.

Active, and in some cases strong,

Trotskyist groups exist today in Europe, Canada, and the United States, throughout southern, middle, and southeast Asia—notably in Ceylon and Burma—in a number of African countries, and in Latin America. What for convenience can be termed the orthodox ones are affiliated with the Fourth International, created in 1938 in opposition both to the Socialist Second International and to the Communist Third International, by then completely under Stalin's control.

From the first, a number of Trotskyist groups in various countries refused to merge with the national sections of the International, either because of personal feuds with their leaders or because the whole idea of a new International seemed unrealistic to them in the existing world context. Others broke loose or were expelled because they were unwilling to follow the rigid party line that the leadership of the International sought to impose in regard to such issues as coexistence, de-Stalinization, the Sino-Soviet rift, support of the Castroite regime in Cuba, or the Soviet occupation of Czechoslovakia. As a result, in most countries today outside the Soviet and Chinese orbits there are several dissident or independent Communist organizations whose competing claims to represent the true principles and spirit of Trotskyism can scarcely be evaluated by outsiders.

Nearly everywhere, it is the student Trotskyists, less concerned with doctrinal quarrels than the veterans are, who are stimulating and leading the general resurgence of Trotskyism. In the process, they are also making a substantial contribution to the student unrest that afflicts most Western nations. "Trotskyist militants . . . were at the origin of the first Western European demonstrations for Vietnam," asserts Pierre Frank in his essay on the Fourth International (of whose secretariat he is a member). "They were in the forefront of the struggle at Berkeley and in the whole anti-war movement in the United States . . ." This somewhat sweeping claim is supported by a liberal British expert on left-wing political affairs, Brian Beedham, in *The Crisis of Communism:* "The student rebellions of the past couple of years—in Paris, Berlin, London, New York—have been led by a curious assortment of people: Maoists, anarchists, and some others who can only be described as fascists of the left. But the most important are the followers of Leon Trotsky."

To avoid attaching undue importance to the conspiratorial aspect of the Trotskyist movement, and thus adopting what Trotsky himself called the "police theory of history," it is well to remember that during their years of wandering in the revolutionary wilderness many Trotskyist groups got into the habit of bolstering their Messianic faith by working within left-wing organizations of greater worldly scope and claiming the results achieved by the host bodies as so many victories for Trotskyism. This glory-by-association technique is too often taken at its face value by official police and intelligence agencies. Moreover, there is a tendency, particularly among youthful Trotskyists, to hail anyone whose political vocabulary is radical, internationalist, and even vaguely Marxist as an ideological brother. Some Trotskyists almost appear to regard Mao as a Trotskyist, although the label would no doubt be indignantly repudiated by the Chinese leader himself. "Che" Guevara is not only a hero to young Trotskyists (as he is to virtually all young radicals today) but is seen by them as an authentically Trotskyist hero—mainly, it seems, because of his militancy and revolutionary ardor.

Whether Trotsky himself, if he were alive, would recognize as his ideological disciples such romantic Marxists as Guevara, and whether he would acknowledge all the victories for Trotskyism claimed by his latter-day adherents, is doubtful but not really material. Clearly, it is not the strict canon of Trotskyist doctrine—if there is such a thing—that captivates the imagination of contemporary youth; even among students who call themselves Trotskyists it seems likely that only a minority have read their master's chief theoretical works.

What, then, explains the current Trotskyist revival throughout the world? Do students and militant young workers admire Trotsky for what he was, or despite what he was? Because of the ideas he stood for, or because of those they *imagine* he stood for?

Some of these questions are relatively easy to answer. Trotsky's historical achievements alone would suffice to elicit the admiration of anyone who professes a revolutionary philosophy. Most objective historians today regard him as the direct artisan of the October Revolution in Russia. He also created the Red Army, without which the Soviet experiment would almost certainly have ended in disaster. Unquestionably, Trotsky was one of the giants of modern history.

Unlike some giants, moreover, he possessed a number of particularly attractive virtues as a human being—courage, integrity, fortitude, intellectual honesty, compassion on occasion, and at least intermittently, a sense of chivalry—along with several all too human failings—vanity, intellectual arrogance, and excessive pugnacity. He was a great writer, a great orator, and a great revolutionary leader. Like Churchill, he made, and wrote, history with an equal sense of style: passionate, intelligent, and a little flamboyant. Politician, scholar, administrator, professional conspirator, writer, historian, social philosopher, distinguished literary critic, brilliant polemicist—Trotsky was probably the nearest the twentieth century has come to producing a universal genius (his chief intellectual weakness was a naive, almost endearing, unawareness of his limitations). His mind was intensely creative, constantly erupting with original ideas, bubbling with energy, magnificently untroubled by its own contradictions.

Other aspects of Trotsky's complex personality and many-sided world outlook seem less calculated to arouse the enthusiasm of young rebels against twentieth-century industrial society. Trotsky was a stern disciplinarian, with himself and with others. An exceptionally devoted and generally faithful husband—at least to his second wife, Natalya Sedova—he was an authoritarian, at times despotic and heartless, father. He was a born rebel, and in theory an ardent lover of human freedom, but repression never troubled his conscience if he felt the success or safety of the revolution was at stake: he slaughtered the anarchist sailors of the Kronstadt naval base in 1921 as ruthlessly as he had earlier slaughtered the White Guards. Though he excoriated Stalin's personal tyranny for years, he believed as strongly as Stalin did, not only in the dictatorship of the proletariat, but in that of the Bolshevik party.

Trotsky was an unabashed militarist, a bureaucratic martinet, a fanatic believer in the virtues of industrialization, and a staunch upholder of Western cultural tradition. He preached—and practiced—the revolutionary virtues of clean appearance, clean living, and clean language. "The struggle against 'foul language,' " he once wrote, "is an essential condition of mental hygiene, just as the fight against filth and vermin is a condition of physical hygiene." In his rare leisure moments Trotsky was a keen outdoorsman, a kind of Marxist Teddy Roosevelt, whose greatest passions after revolution and literature were hunting and fishing.

Though some young Trotskyists may be happily ignorant of the "square" and authoritarian elements in their prophet's teachings, it does not seem too farfetched to suggest that a larger number are positively attracted by these elements and are therefore unconsciously revolting against the current permissiveness of Western society rather than against its imagined repressiveness. There is a similar but even stronger case for thinking that the unavowed, sometimes inverted, romanticism of Trotsky's life and character accounts for much of his appeal to a certain type of contemporary young rebel. Trotsky was often accused of being a romantic Marxist; there is no doubt that to the end of his days he remained a Marxist romantic.

Revolutionaries commonly grow up in families that are either harshly exploited or else overprivileged, and romantics spring more often from a decadent or dispossessed elite than from an ascendant social milieu. Trotsky —originally Lev (Leon) Davidovich Bronstein—was born, however, on a farm in the southern Ukraine of parents who had started poor but were making it, by their own efforts. They were Jews, but they lived as independent, landowning peasants—a rare thing among Russian Jews at that time—and were largely free both from the trammels of custom that Jewish society imposed upon itself and from the restrictions or vexations that the czarist state imposed upon Russian Jewry.

Life in the Bronstein family when Leon was born, in 1879, was not very different in many respects from what it might have been had the family lived at the same period in Kansas or Nebraska. They had clay floors in two of the rooms, several hundred acres of good wheatland, and a free horizon. Leon's father, David Leontievich, drove himself and his family as hard as he drove his workers. He eventually set up a prosperous flour mill in addition to his farm and was respected by his peasant customers for being honest and tightfisted.

When he was nine, Leon was sent to school in Odessa. He lived with middle-class relations of his mother named Spentzer. They were cultivated and mildly liberal Jewish intellectuals, who recognized Leon's exceptional gifts from the start and systematically helped him to develop them. He became regularly the top boy in his class, but got into trouble more than once for defying school regulations or being rude to his teachers.

Young Bronstein moved to the Black Sea port of Nikolayev for his last year of secondary school. It was there he first got caught up in the student revolutionary movement. What pushed him into it is not wholly clear. The sympathy with the underdog that was later to become one of his ruling passions seems at that time to have manifested itself only fitfully. Probably the deep-rooted emotional allergy to authority that he manifested all his life was activated by the general climate of rebellion then prevailing in Russian student circles, itself a reaction to the intensified despotism that had characterized the reign of Nicholas II during its first years.

Whatever his initial motivations, Bronstein's revolutionary career began under appropriately romantic auspices. He was introduced by school friends into a radical discussion group conducted by a self-educated Czech gardener named Franz Shvigovsky. Though the group's subversive activities were limited to tea drinking and talk, Shvigovsky was regarded as a dangerous conspirator by the czarist police, and therefore had immense prestige in the eyes of the students.

One member of the group was a young woman, several years older than Bronstein, named Alexandra Sokolovskaya. Alexandra—who later became Bronstein's first wife—was a Marxist. Bronstein, like his mentor, Shvigovsky, thought of himself as a Narodnik, a socialist-populist of the old-fashioned, idealistic, warmhearted Russian sort. "A curse upon all Marxists, and upon those who want to bring dryness and hardness into all the relations of life," he exclaimed in a defiant New Year's toast, addressed with adolescent boorishness to Alexandra herself. She walked out of the room, and a few months later he became a convert to Marxism.

This incident illustrates the basic dichotomy in Trotsky's nature. There were to be occasions in his career as an adult revolutionary when the Marxist zealot or windy theorizer would

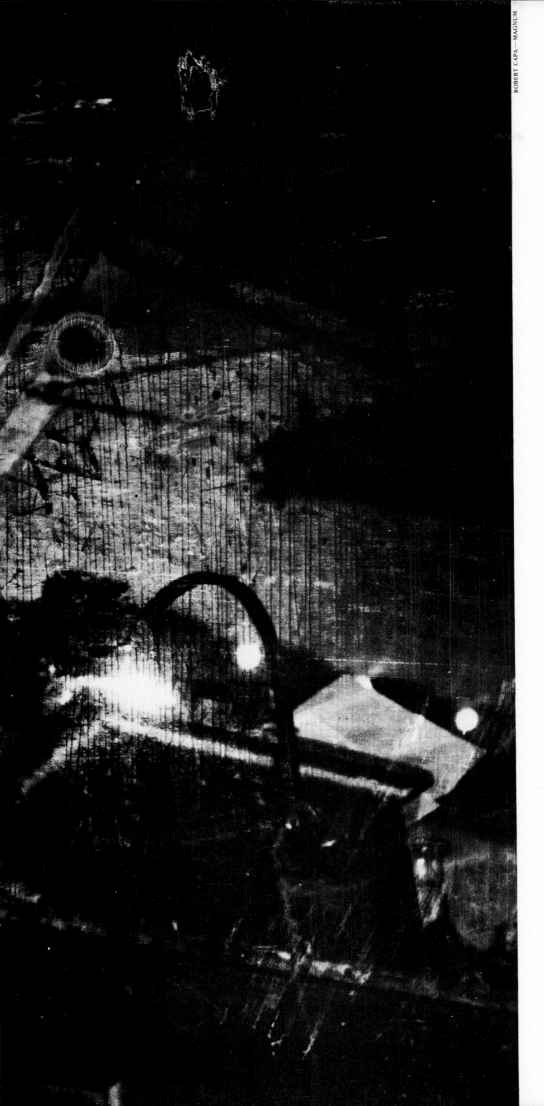

seem, in fact, to have forgotten his native humanity, not to mention his common sense. (In 1919 Trotsky proposed conscripting workers to lay the basis for a socialist economy in Russia, and in what a few years later would have seemed a typical example of Stalinist cynicism, denounced the "wretched and miserable liberal prejudice" that forced labor was always unproductive.) More often, perhaps, Trotsky's Marxism would serve as a focusing lens to the somewhat diffuse ardor of his temperament, magnifying both his virtues and his faults to a heroic intensity, ultimately enabling him to personify better than any other figure in modern history the twentieth-century myth of revolution.

Young Bronstein went to jail for revolutionary agitation for the first time a few months after his eighteenth birthday. (He had briefly attended the University of Odessa—where his professors had predicted a brilliant future for him as a pure mathematician—and then dropped out to return to Nikolayev as an underground agitator.) He spent two years in various prisons before being sentenced to exile in Siberia. After another two years he escaped, getting away from Siberia on a false passport—in which he had written, for the first time, the name Trotsky —and leaving behind a wife and two baby daughters. (He had married Alexandra Sokolovskaya in prison while still a minor.)

Sent abroad as the delegate of the Social Democratic underground in Siberia, Trotsky, then twenty-three, joined the émigré circle around Lenin in London and began contributing to Lenin's paper, *Iskra*. A priority objective of Marxist revolutionaries in those days, as now, was to discredit liberals and moderates, especially in the eyes of the

Exiled by Stalin, Trotsky gives an impassioned speech to students in Copenhagen in 1932. Trotsky was then living on the Turkish island of Prinkipo, once a place of banishment reserved for Byzantine empresses. This was Robert Capa's first published photograph.

young. Trotsky, with his youthful verve and insolence, his bent towards sarcasm, and his genius for invective, excelled in this activity, particularly as an orator addressing various Social Democratic gatherings.

Soon, however, the young iconoclast turned the cutting edge of his tongue and pen against Lenin himself. Trotsky believed in a centrally controlled revolutionary party and recognized the need on occasion for conspiratorial methods, but he criticized Lenin for trying to centralize too much control in his own hands and for substituting professionalized conspiracy for mass action. Relations between the two men became ambivalent, each esteeming but censuring the other, and remained that way until 1917, when Trotsky finally accepted Lenin's primacy as a revolutionary leader. In the quarrel between Bolsheviks and Mensheviks that split the Russian Social Democratic party after 1903, Trotsky most frequently adopted an independent position, more extremist—in the revolutionary sense—than that of the Mensheviks, but more democratic than that of the Bolsheviks.

Trotsky slipped back into Russia as the Revolution of 1905 was beginning, and it catapulted him to fame, at least within the revolutionary movement, at the age of twenty-six. No other Marxist émigré, not even Lenin himself, and few underground militants assessed the situation so fast and so accurately, or manifested so much "revolutionary intuition"—to use Trotsky's own term—in exploiting it. Elected to the St. Petersburg Soviet (Council) of Workers' Deputies, Trotsky almost immediately became its dominant figure. He simultaneously made himself popular with the mass of Petersburg workers as a rabble-rousing balcony orator and kept a tight rein on the hotheads in the soviet who deluded themselves with the hope of storming some czarist Bastille or dreamed of a heroic death on the barricades.

When the czar's police finally moved against the soviet, Trotsky, who was chairing its last meeting, instructed his fellow delegates to break the hammers of their revolvers before surrendering, gave the floor to the police commander so that he could read out the warrant of arrest, and then told the baffled official to keep quiet while the meeting wound up its agenda. The performance was pure Trotsky—and wonderful revolutionary theatre.

While in prison awaiting trial, which led to a new deportation to Siberia and shortly afterward to a new escape abroad, Trotsky wrote a pamphlet outlining a radical, and to some, heretical, innovation in Marxist doctrine: the theory of the Permanent Revolution, which became the cornerstone of Trotskyism. Briefly summarized, the theory stipulated: (1) that despite Russia's industrial backwardness, the country's relatively small proletariat could and should impose its leadership on the peasant majority in the revolution against czarism; (2) that because of the dominant role of the proletariat this revolution would finally turn into a socialist one, drastically shortening, if not skipping over, the bourgeois-democratic phase predicted by most orthodox Marxists at the time; (3) that the Russian proletariat would not be able to remain long in power without the massive support of the European proletariat, thus implying revolution in Europe; and (4) that the Russian workers by their example and by throwing Russia's "colossal" power into the scales of the class struggle abroad could initiate a successful world-wide socialist revolution or series of revolutions.

The global aspects of the theory of Permanent Revolution seem most pertinent, if still questionable, today; they have undoubtedly influenced revolutionary leadership in China, Cuba, and elsewhere in the Third World. In 1906, however, it was the assumption that a revolution led by the working class was possible and desirable in Russia that startled, and frequently shocked, European Marxists. Indeed, Trotsky's pamphlet marked an important date not only in Marxist but in world intellectual history. It was the bluntest, if not the first, repudiation by a Social Democrat of the traditional Marxist revolutionary credo that the workers should seek to seize power only when they had become a majority of the nation. Lenin himself had not yet moved so far on the road that was to lead from the dictatorship of the proletariat to the dictatorship of the Communist party and finally of the party's apparat.

After the triumph of the Bolsheviks, Trotsky's theory of the Permanent Revolution furnished in large measure the ideological background for the split between him and Stalin. Overshadowed at first by personal antagonisms and quarrels over more immediate issues of policy, the Permanent Revolution eventually became in Stalin's eyes his adversary's major heresy. Perhaps it was the only point of pure doctrine in dispute between him and Trotsky in regard to which the cynical Georgian had any deep convictions.

What mainly caused the trouble was not Trotsky's overoptimistic expectation that the Russian revolution would start an almost immediate and irresistible chain reaction of revolution in Europe—most of the other Bolshevik leaders shared this delusion—but the corollary that Trotsky derived from the eventual exposure of his malcalculation. The revolutionary timetable would have to be revised, Trotsky admitted, but the long-range promotion of socialist revolution throughout the world should remain the basis of Soviet policy. True socialism could not come into being in Russia until the whole world was socialist. To put world revolution out of one's mind and concentrate on building socialism in one country would inevitably produce "bureaucratic deformations" that betrayed the Marxist ideal.

As the foremost champion and theorist of Socialism in One Country, particularly with the collapse of the German and Chinese revolutions after the First World War, Stalin naturally found Trotsky's viewpoint abhorrent.

As the rift between them widened, Stalin worked up an elaborate demonology that portrayed Trotsky as a secret saboteur of the revolution and Trotskyism as the predestined counter-revolutionary fruit of his alleged original "Menshevism."

On Trotsky's side, the doctrine of Permanent Revolution gradually merged with his criticisms of the Soviet state bureaucracy and his protests against the stifling of internal democracy within the Communist party; together, they would lay the foundations for his almost equally metaphysical dogma of the Revolution Betrayed. Stalinism, as he finally came to view it, was not a personal aberration but the epitome of those very "bureaucratic deformations" inevitably generated by the victory of Socialism in One Country over the Permanent Revolution. Of course, Trotsky could not—or at least, did not—foresee the emergence of Stalinism when he formulated his theory of the Permanent Revolution in 1906. If he had, he might have theorized somewhat more cautiously about the desirability of attempting to establish the dictatorship of the proletariat in a country that had just begun to produce a working class. (That any kind of dictatorship tends sooner or later to degenerate into a personal despotism never seems to have occurred to him.)

Trotsky was still in exile (in New York at the time) when the March Revolution overthrew the czarist regime in 1917. He rushed back to begin mobilizing the Russian, and world, proletariat for the final struggle. In Petrograd he met Lenin, by now converted to the doctrine of the Permanent Revolution, or something very similar, and the two men patched up their fifteen-year-old feud. After a few weeks Trotsky joined the Bolshevik party and became the chief executor of Lenin's insurrectionary program, though the politico-military strategy of the insurrection seems to have been largely his own. Elected president of the Petrograd Soviet in September, Trotsky brilliantly exploited his official position to organize the armed Bolshevik uprising behind a smoke screen of revolutionary oratory that bemused both the Kerensky government and a number of his brother socialists.

The most vivid and detailed account of Trotsky's role in the October Revolution is that given by Trotsky himself in his two masterpieces, *My Life* and *The History of the Russian Revolution.* In both books he seems much of the time to be occupying the front of history's stage, but on the basis of all the available evidence, he had every right to put himself there. He is frank, at moments cynical, in revealing the deception and covert manipulations that lay behind the Bolshevik coup (". . . an insurrection . . . develops better, the more it looks like self-defense").

The insurrection, however, as it emerges from the magic of Trotsky's prose, was no mere *Putsch.* It had to be conspired, but it was not simply a conspiracy. It was largely a military stroke, but the soldiers of the Petrograd garrison who carried it out had already been won over by the "proletarian vanguard." What Trotsky means is that Bolshevik agitators had systematically subverted the loyalty of the garrison with revolutionary propaganda; he himself was the party's foremost agitator, and his volcanic oratory almost literally mesmerized the crowds, civilian or military, that were exposed to it. No doubt he mesmerized himself.

In plotting successfully to seize power from Kerensky, Trotsky did not consider that he and Lenin had themselves made a revolution; he insisted—not always convincingly—that they had merely helped one to be born, acting as midwives to history. And what history was bringing forth with their aid was not just a Russian revolution but the Russian prologue to a world revolution that was destined almost overnight to transform the human condition. The Permanent Revolution was theory in 1906; by October, 1917, it had become Messianic mystique.

Consciously, or almost consciously, Trotsky came to regard himself as the prophet of this revolutionary mystique, uniquely qualified—especially after Lenin's death—to interpret its revelation. At a deeper level of his mind, especially in moments of supreme crisis, when there was no time for rational analysis and "revolutionary intuition" took over, he seemed rather to be identifying himself with the hero of some epic myth of revolution that his own imagination had conceived. He became charged with elemental energy; it was as if invisible sparks were incessantly crackling from his heavy mustache, his defiantly satanic goatee, and his wild shock of hair.

The attitudes he struck took on not merely a theatrical but an archetypal quality. His actions had an exemplary and an almost ritualistic, as well as a practical, dimension. When he spoke on certain particularly dramatic occasions, he became the voice of the revolution itself. "To the dustbin of history!" he shouted at the old Menshevik leader Theodore Dan, who was protesting in the Congress of Soviets against the Bolshevik insurrection, and it was all the young, impatient, implacable todays since the beginning of time shouting down the tired, timid, old yesterdays.

The element of heroic myth in Trotsky's career was no less marked during the Russian Civil War, when as the Soviet Commissar for War he lived for more than two years in his famous armored train (usually only the locomotive was armored), dashing from one threatened front to another. His personal contribution to the formation of the Red Army and to its victory on several decisive battlefields was undoubtedly immense, but his contribution to revolutionary legend was even greater.

Trotsky's train was a rolling liaison office between the Soviet government in Moscow and the fighting fronts, plus a communications center, emergency supply depot, and psychological-warfare unit. In the economic breakdown and general chaos that prevailed throughout Russia after the civil war erupted, following the October Revolution and defeat in the war with Germany, it was a brilliant administrative improvisation. Trotsky's personal role as an ambulatory war minister was not purely that of a civilian administrator, however, and his constant visits to the front lines or outposts, accompanied by members of his own bodyguard, wearing leather jackets with distinctive brass insignia, were more dramatic than the usual VIP morale-building battlefield tours.

At one particularly critical moment in czarist General Yudenich's offensive against Petrograd, which narrowly failed to capture the former capital, the commander of a Red regiment, hard pressed by the advancing Whites, ordered an injudicious withdrawal that put the neighboring units in jeopardy. Trotsky, who happened to be visiting that sector at the time, recognized the danger. Leaping on a horse that was standing nearby, he galloped forward to countermand the order for retreat, rounded up the stragglers who were continuing to flee, and—still mounted on his providential charger—led the regiment back to its original position under enemy fire.

The chapters in *My Life* on the civil war almost give the impression at times that it was won by sheer heroism and force of will, with Trotsky as a revolutionary Prometheus inspiring the soldiers of the Red Army to defy all "pusillanimous historical fatalism"— an odd phrase from the pen of a Marxist writer. The same romantic subjectivism that colored Trotsky's writing as a military historian undoubtedly distorted his judgment as a revolutionary strategist on occasion. In his preoccupation with morale and psychological impact (Trotsky was one of the master propagandists of his age), he tended to overlook Napoleon's "big battalions." As the chief Soviet negotiator at Brest-Litovsk, he wanted to reject the outrageous German peace terms and adopt a policy of "no peace and no

war." Though fine revolutionary propaganda, the policy, as Lenin realized, would probably have resulted in the replacement of the Soviet regime by a German military government.

What Lenin termed Trotsky's "excessive self-confidence" likewise tempted him sometimes into rash courses of action. He was by no means, however, the irresponsible hothead that Stalinist critics have made him out to be. He was more prudent and realistic than Lenin himself, for example, in opposing the march on Warsaw during the war with Poland in 1920. Despite his obsession with the Permanent Revolution, Trotsky argued that the Polish masses would not welcome the invaders and that in the absence of local political support, attempting the military conquest of Poland would be a reckless adventure. The disastrous outcome confirmed his prescience.

Trotsky was seldom too much the revolutionary doctrinaire to reject a favorable tactical alliance with one ideological enemy against another: he was probably the chief Soviet sponsor of the Rapallo policy of an entente with German nationalism against the Versailles powers. His usual reaction in the face of overwhelming force, however, was to avoid a suicidal confrontation while waging an incessant war of harassment and psychological attrition against the adversary, at the risk of provoking disastrous reprisals. (The same strategic pattern can be detected in the permanent war that present-day Trotskyists wage against bourgeois society. So far, the results have not been particularly brilliant—except, perhaps, to those of Trotsky's spiritual heirs for whom the struggle is its own reward.)

A normal postrevolutionary career as bureaucrat and statesman in the Soviet Union might have dimmed to some extent the revolutionary glamour that surrounds Trotsky's name today. Stalin saved Trotsky from this fate by outmaneuvering him in the power struggles within the Bolshevik party

Closely guarded by Mexican police, Trotsky in plus fours stands with his wife, his friend the painter Diego Rivera (right), and an unidentified follower in the garden of his villa outside Mexico City in 1940. In May of that year Soviet agents, armed with machine guns and led by the painter David Siqueiros, had raided the villa, but their assassination attempt was thwarted. Three months later, another GPU agent, who was posing as Trotsky's friend, killed the sixty-one-year-old revolutionary with a pickaxe.

that followed Lenin's death in 1924 and by eventually banishing him from the USSR. The personal dictatorship Stalin established likewise furnished Trotsky with the subsidiary myth—the Revolution Betrayed—that helped insulate his central myth of world revolution from too brutal exposure to historical reality. Finally, by sending an assassin to Mexico to strike down his exiled enemy in 1940, Stalin unwittingly supplied the last touch needed to consecrate in the minds of Trotsky's disciples, and of disciples to come, the image of the mythological hero fulfilling his tragic destiny.

It would be a distortion of contemporary history, as well as an affront to the memory of a great man, to imply that the romantic and mythological elements in Trotsky's life, and the element of mystique in his doctrine, suffice to explain the present revival of Trotskyism among young people throughout the world. (Its genuine internationalism is certainly part of its appeal.) But perhaps among today's crop of young Trotskyists, and no doubt other rebels, there are a certain number whose unconscious need for a hero to worship is even stronger than their conscious attachment to the cause of revolution. That is a disturbing thought from one viewpoint, but a reassuring one from another.

Edmond Taylor went to France in the 1930's as a foreign correspondent, and with breaks for world upheavals, has lived there ever since. His memoir Awakening from History *was published by Gambit.*

Part of the medieval Pilgrim's Way to Canterbury Cathedral, route of Chaucer's taletelling travelers, survives today as a public footpath in Kent.

Whan that Aprille
with his shoures sote
The droghte of Marche hath perced to the rote
And bathed every veyne in swich licour
Of which vertu engendred is the flour...
Than longen folk to goon on pilgrimages

At this moment of writing, a musical version of Chaucer's *Canterbury Tales* is playing in London, and after two years it shows no signs of diminishing popularity. It is, on the whole, a pretty bad adaptation: the songs are tuneless, the lines lack the medieval gusto of Chaucer's original, and there is an air of sniggering lubricity about the production. The pleasure the audience gets from this enstaged and watered-down Chaucer is one of sanctioned naughtiness—the action teetering on the brink of open fornication, the lines peppered with "fart" and "arse," but every obscenity made respectable, even holy, by the awareness that this is Ancient Literature, a Classic, part of the English Heritage. But these audiences are hardly likely to be led on to the real thing, to the complex soul and language of an England as foreign as Red China, and far more revolutionary.

The Canterbury Tales was probably designed about 1387, when Geoffrey Chaucer was in his early forties. One cannot be more specific than that, since there is no question of a publication date. William Caxton, the first English printer, was not born until about 1421 —some twenty years after Chaucer's death—and his Westminster printing press was not set up until 1476. One of his first printing tasks was, indeed, *The Canterbury Tales,* but the great work was known only in manuscript until then. So the terms we associate with literary masterpieces—"popularity," "innumerable editions," "best seller," and so on—do not apply to Chaucer.

Like all medieval literary men, Chaucer wrote for pleasure—his own and that of his friends—in his spare time. Of this there could have been little, for Chaucer was not an aristocratic rentier. He had to earn his bread, but he was lucky enough to earn it among the cultivated—men like the Duke of Clarence, John of Gaunt, eventually the king himself. By *the king*

we mean, of course, three kings: Edward III, that great roaring ravager of France; the delicate and ill-fated Richard II, son of the Black Prince; and his usurper, Henry IV. Chaucer went on diplomatic missions; he served in the army and was taken prisoner (though soon ransomed); later he took on the big job of controller of customs for the Port of London. In 1372 he seems to have been sent on a royal mission to Genoa and Florence, and he may have met two fellow poets—Boccaccio and Petrarch—in one place or the other. That he was influenced in his writing by these two exquisite craftsmen we certainly know. *The Canterbury Tales* is a close cousin of Boccaccio's *Decameron;* the courtly delicacy of some of Chaucer's lyrics owes much to Petrarch. But Chaucer remained, in an age that in many ways was far more internationally-minded than our own, an English writer, not an imitation Frenchman or Italian. Even more than that, he remained a London writer.

By ANTHONY BURGESS

KNIGHT

In our day we care little about the provenance of an author. He may come from Liverpool, from St. Ives or Milwaukee, from Dublin or Johannesburg, and to us he is essentially a practitioner of the English language. The English language, despite its regional differences, is now what it was not in Chaucer's day—a unified and homogeneous medium. In Chaucer's England, English consisted of a number of dialects, which, because of geographic isolation, tended to be mutually incomprehensible. To some extent this segmentation of English still obtains, in America as in England, but only on the spoken level; in Chaucer's time the variety of English applied as much to the written word as to the spoken.

Read *The Canterbury Tales*, and than tackle *Sir Gawain and the Green Knight*. They come from the same century, but the fact that one is in London English and the other in Cheshire English renders the gap between them bridgeable only by the scholar. Chaucer's English is a dialect, but it happened to be a lucky dialect. The dialect of London has become the language of all educated speakers of English. We have to approach *Gawain* as a book in a foreign tongue; we recognize in the *Tales* an earlier form of our own language, and of Shakespeare's, and Joyce's, and Mailer's, and Bellow's.

To be exact, Chaucer's English belonged to a bigger swath of England than just the capital. We call it East Midland English, acknowledging that it was also the language of counties like Oxfordshire and Cambridgeshire—far enough away from London—as well as of the counties (Middlesex, Surrey, Kent) that share the great city. We may say that three elements determined the

pre-eminence of this dialect: the existence of important centers of learning at Oxford and Cambridge, the commercial and political greatness of London, and the fact that a great poet wrote in it. When G. K. Chesterton said that Chaucer created the king's English, he was exaggerating, but, as in all his exaggerations, there was a kernel of truth in it. Chaucer showed for the first time the artistic potentialities of East Midland English and made it thereafter, for America as well as for England, the only linguistic medium a serious writer could decently use.

ead the opening of the Prologue to the *Tales,* and to the eye at least, there will seem little substantial difference from the English used in present-day America and the British Commonwealth:

Whan that Aprille with his shoures sote
The droghte of Marche hath perced to the rote,
And bathed every veyne in swich licour,
Of which vertu engendred is the flour . . .

Pronunciation, of course, is a different matter. The vowels are close to French and Italian; the *gh* of "droghte" is a throaty rasp, not a mere vowel-length signal; the *r* is a virile roll. The *e* at the end of a word is usually given full value, except when it's swallowed up by another vowel coming right after it, and this is responsible for a kind of Franco-Italian lightness that has disappeared from a language that is now somewhat heavy-footed, and let's confess it, Teutonically assertive. Milton, whose English was virtually identical with our own, could write

As the gay motes that people the Sun Beams . . .

and fail to convey the insubstantiality. Chaucer's corresponding line is all light and air:

As thikke as motes in the sonne-beem . . .

The language of *The Canterbury Tales* is the language of a man learned in all the arts and sciences of his day, including the important art of courtliness, but it is not the language of a snob or a pedant. The heartening thing

about the Middle Ages, as that long and complex period is expressed in Chaucer, is what T. S. Eliot would call a community of sensibility: the aristocratic intellect does not despise the grosser plebeian sensorium. Chaucer can accommodate knights and priests and officers of the crown, and also cooks and millers and carpenters—ladies and gentlemen, and also men and women. The high romance of the Knight's Tale is balanced by the coarseness of the Miller's Tale, and the prissiness of the Prioress is answered by the Wife of Bath, who anticipates Rabelais. The language of court and street and kitchen is coaxed into verse patterns, but it remains living speech, matching the living characters.

These characters are perhaps the first real men and women (or ladies and gentlemen) in English literature. Earlier writers—including the author or authors of our first English epic, *Beowulf*—were more concerned with violence and morality than with the human soul and body. Chaucer, a poet, is also a novelist. His characters are as credible and as memorable as any in Shakespeare and Dickens, although they are presented as types rather than as individuals. Most of them lack Christian names, but none lack named trades or offices. And yet they are, in spite of their generalized presentation, as powerfully individuated as Falstaff or Uriah Heep.

There are from twenty-nine to thirty-three characters—the text is unclear as to exactly how many. Representative of all the trades and civil and ecclesiastical offices of fourteenth-century England, they assemble in the Prologue at the Tabard Inn in South-

WIFE OF BATH

MILLER

wark, London, before traveling in a democratic company to the shrine of St. Thomas à Becket at Canterbury. Is such a pilgrimage really plausible? We find it hard to imagine a similar group in present-day Christendom. We have to think in terms of a film star, a tycoon, a bishop, a bank clerk, a middle-aged pub cleaner, a short-order hash-slinger, a debt collector, a known fraud, an antique-furniture faker, a possible prostitute, and a published poet, as well as a number of other representative citizens of America or England, getting together in a second-class hotel and traveling in a chartered bus to say their prayers in a church sanctified by a political martyrdom. The mind, as they say, boggles. Lourdes might be a different matter, being the lodestone of desperate invalids. But Chaucer's pilgrims are fit, beefy men and women, very much in the world. What have they to do with an arduous road journey to a national shrine? What is in it for them?

There is little point in our talking of medieval superstition. Chaucer's age was as scientific and as rational as our own. It did not go in for horoscopy and table rapping; it was not especially devout. St. Thomas à Becket was not even glamorized by having recently been in the news. His murder had no topical appeal; he had been struck down by Henry II's four drunken knights a good two centuries earlier. Even his canonization, which came two years after his martyrdom, had lost that special halo of national pride that attaches to the knowledge of having an ambassador in heaven. Still, England had a saint at Canterbury, and he was as good as any of Italy or France. But why bother to seek his shrine?

Chaucer, in the first lines of his Pro-

logue, takes it for granted that sweet-showering April is the month when "longen folk to goon on pilgrimages." Translate this into secular terms and we become aware of that perennial call of the road that animates each of us at the end of the long northern winter. But consider how claustrophobic that winter was during the Middle Ages— the roads bad at any time but totally impassable when the snows came and February rains followed. "The droghte of Marche" parched the surfaces, the rains that fell in April were intermittent and "sote," or sweet. The birds returned, the virtue of the liquor from the sky engendered spring flowers. Joy in the earth's renewal is perhaps the primal religious emotion; combine it with pleasure at being able to once more take to the road and roam the world, and you have the palmer's urge, the humble elation of the pilgrim. Clinging to the hearth throughout the winter, our view of human society shrinks somewhat. With spring it can become expansive again; in London a knight who has come from France can talk of his adventures to a lady from Bath, a west-coast shipwright, and a prioress from Stratford-atte-Bowe. This Canterbury pilgrimage seems the most reasonable thing in the world.

rom an artistic point of view, Chaucer's motive in bringing together this diversity of single-aimed men and women is to provide a pretext for telling stories. Harry Bailey, landlord of the Tabard, considers that the journey —on which he will accompany them— will be sweetened if each pilgrim tells four tales, two on the outward journey and two on the return. Whichever tale-teller does best will be rewarded with a free supper when they all get back to the Tabard. This is an ingenious means of unifying diversity, of creating a genuine whole instead of a mere parcel of disparate tales. Giovanni Boccaccio was rather less ingenious in his *Decameron.* He sent a company of young, aristocratic men and women to a coun-

try estate to escape from the plague in Florence (the Black Death that Chaucer had seen ravage England), and set them to beguile the time with story-telling. Chaucer does more; he puts the scheme into literal motion and promises us (though he died before he could fulfill the promise) a mildly thrilling conclusion. He is very English in bringing in a sporting element, as well as in putting the tales on horseback. But his true advance on Boccaccio lies in his insistence on the characterization of the storytellers and on the diversity of this characterization. Boccaccio's aristocrats are of the same class, face, and voice. Chaucer's men and women are sharply contrasted individually as well as socially, and—here is the biggest advance of all—the stories they tell are wholly in character.

Like Shakespeare, Chaucer was not greatly interested in the invention of plot. He took his themes from other authors, including Boccaccio, and from the complementary stockpots of classical and popular legend. His achievement, like that of most great writers, lies in his highly personal treatment of common, or not so common, literary property. To say what *The Canterbury Tales* is about is, perhaps, not to say much about Chaucer. The wit, the skill, and the pathos are not detachable from the lines he wrote, and these lines are not best served by being presented as dishes of canapés. He is capable of the epigrammatic thrust, the brief unforgettable summation ("Murder will out" is his, as well as "The smiler with the knife under the cloak"), but he is essentially a writer to be taken in leisurely meals or, if you prefer, long drinking bouts. But to say something

TEXT CONTINUED ON PAGE 57

MERCHANT

47

A Canterbury Album

On the following eight pages, Zevi Blum, a French-born architect and water-colorist, provides new illustrations for five of the most famous Canterbury Tales. *In the lines of his compositions he has tried to capture the "Byzantine melodrama" he finds in the stories.*

The Wife of Bath, opposite, hefty, hearty, and self-confident, has a tale to tell that is well suited to her own lusty experience: the story of a knight who discovers that a man's recipe for marital bliss is to submit to the "sovereignty" of his wife. By her own account, the Wife of Bath has practiced what she preached, having bullied, bossed, and buried five husbands with her sexual appetites and her equally debilitating harangues. In Blum's picture, the widow has the shoulders and calves of a fullback. Whip held under her ample skirt, she is, as she well knows, the living refutation of all official medieval doctrines about the authority of husbands and the submissiveness of wives.

The Man of Law's Tale concerns the virtuous Constance, long-lost daughter of a Roman emperor, who suffers numerous Job-like misfortunes that cannot shake her Christian fortitude. Blum's illustration, overleaf, depicts the moment when the meek heroine, center, finds herself standing trial on a false charge of murder in the faraway kingdom of Northumberland. The real murderer is a wicked knight whose advances she has spurned and who has just testified on oath that Constance is guilty. At that very moment, however, divine Providence strikes the armored knight dead and causes his eyeballs to start out of his head. Seeing the miracle, the king, at left, sets Constance free.

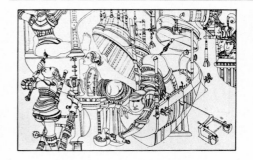

The Miller's Tale is a ribald farce about an old carpenter, his compliant young wife, Alison, their boarder, Nicholas, and a foppish suitor, Absolon. At the story's end the carpenter is sleeping in a tub he has hung from the ceiling, having been persuaded by Nicholas that a second Flood is imminent. After Alison and Nicholas make love, Absolon asks at the window for a kiss, and Alison obliges by presenting her naked rump. Outraged, Absolon returns with a hot iron and asks for a second kiss. This time, Nicholas pretends to be Alison and is duly taken aback for his wit. Hearing the screams, the husband thinks the Flood has come, cuts the ropes, and tumbles ignominiously to the floor.

The Merchant's Tale is another story of a foolish old man, January (left), who weds a young girl, May, shown here in her marriage bed. Fearing the worst, the priest (at right) pointedly bids the bride to be faithful to her vows. Later, January goes blind and jealously insists that May stay in physical contact with him at all times. The sly May, however, arranges a tryst with her lover in a pear tree, evading the rule by standing in the tree on her husband's back. Incensed by the ruse, the god Pluto restores January's sight. But May has a ready excuse: she has been in a tree with a man, she says, trying to cure January's blindness. All—perhaps temporarily—is forgiven.

The Friar's Tale concerns a church official, a summoner, who uses his power to bring fornicators to justice as a means to extort money. One day the rascal meets a man as rascally as he, who turns out to be the Devil—a quiverful of arrows lies across his back in Blum's illustration. An old woman, one of the summoner's innocent victims, cries out to him angrily: "The Devil take your body"; the Devil obliges and the summoner goes to Hell. In transforming the woman's house in this tale, and the tubs in the Miller's Tale, into strange mechanical devices, Blum seems to suggest the intricate machinery of melodrama in the tales of the Canterbury pilgrims.

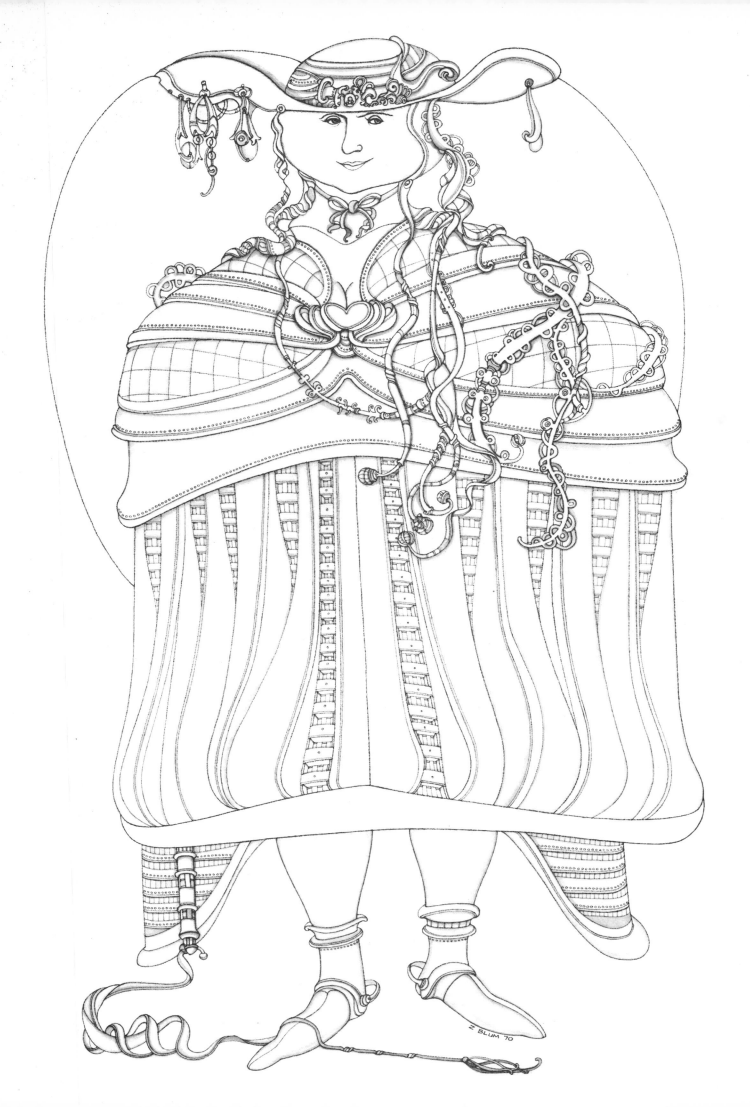

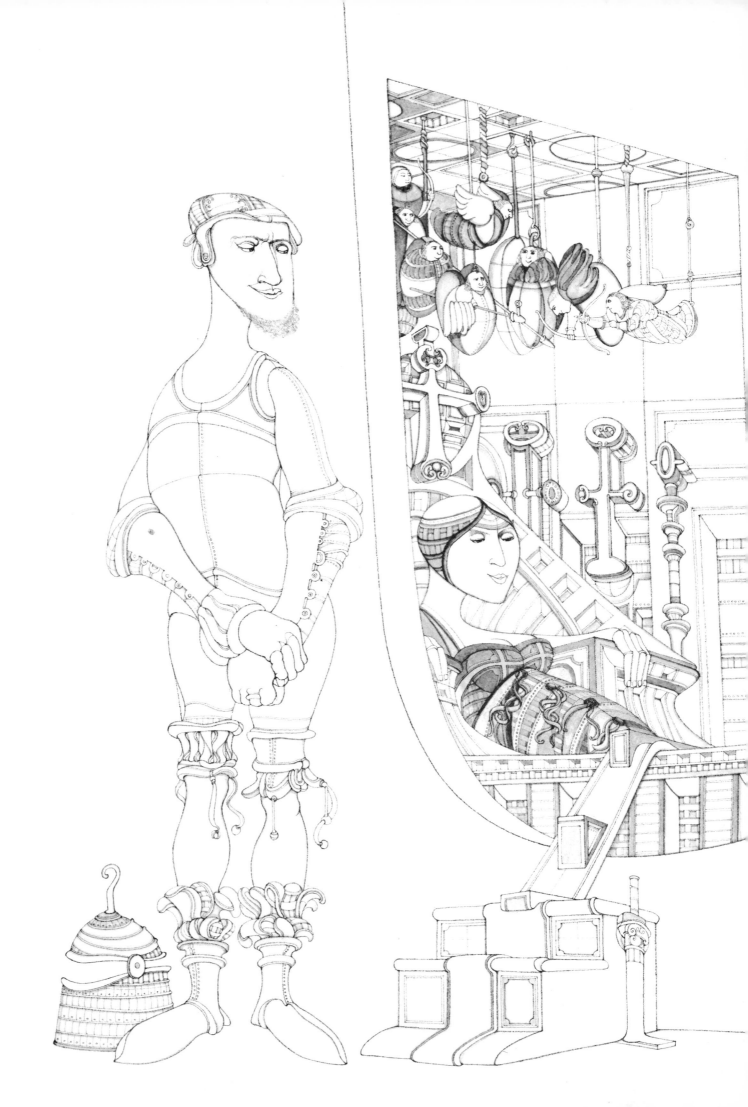

TEXT CONTINUED FROM PAGE 47

of the content of the tales is to say something about the preoccupations of an educated, tolerant, liberal mind of fourteenth-century England.

The Knight's Tale is taken from the *Teseida*—or *Thesaid*—of Boccaccio. This was an epic about the hero Theseus, king of Athens, and his wife Hippolyta, queen of the Amazons. Chaucer's concern is with the rivalry between Palamon and Arcite, prisoners of Theseus, for the love of Emilia, sister of Hippolyta. It is a classical theme, converted to medieval romance by the introduction of courtly love and a fine swingeing tournament between the competing lovers. Shakespeare must have glanced at this tale when he started planning *A Midsummer Night's Dream*, just as he must have dipped into Chaucer's *Troilus and Criseyde* for his own bitter version of that love tale of the Trojan War.

This sad, noble, essentially chivalric, story of Palamon and Arcite is followed at once—a scherzo after the first expansive movement of a symphony— by the ribald Miller's Tale, which is a kind of leisurely dirty story. A double sexual deception takes place that is worthy of Feydeau and much more brisk. A student is hotly attracted to a carpenter's wife. He gets the carpenter out of the way by convincing him that a second Flood is coming and that he'd better find tubs for them to stay in during the night of the Flood. But the carpenter's wife has another admirer— a clerk who demands a kiss at the window just as the student begins his fornicatory work. It is dark, and the wife presents her fundament, which the rival kisses "ful savourly." But, going away, still smacking his lips, he reflects that women do not usually have beards. He returns for, ostensibly, another kiss, but he brings with him a red-hot iron. This time the student presents *his* bottom. The clerk's yell as he "brende so his toute" is heartrending: the carpenter, sleeping in the small tub that he has suspended from the rafters, awakes believing that the Flood has started. He cuts his cables

PARDONER

and shipwrecks on the floor. Curtain.

The miller who tells this tale is not only a coarse man but, in Chaucer's words, a man with "a thumb of gold." This means that in weighing the grain he has milled from the villagers' corn, he keeps his thumb on the scale. Too many millers gained villainous gold in this way, and yet there was only one miller to a rural community: what could the poor small holder do? One answer comes in the tale of the Reeve, or bailiff, who is the next to entertain the company. He has a double motive for telling the story of a miller who is sexually duped, since, like the poor naufraged man in the Miller's Tale, he has himself been a carpenter. And, like everybody else, he has suffered from cheating millers. His story tells how two clerks (which means primarily men who can read and write and secondarily men in holy orders) "swive" the wife and daughter of a miller who has robbed them of part of their grain.

here is conflict of character proceeding now, a humorous dialectic in counterpoint to the stories. Chaucer is good-humoredly satirizing a small social wrong in the manner of a television comedian; he is also warning us to expect satire that goes beyond mere cheating millers.

REEVE

The fourteenth century was a time of dissatisfaction with irregularities in the Church. Too many of the clergy cultivated wealth and neglected their pastoral commitments in favor of the fleshpots; the secular power of the priests was deeply resented, and not only by the laity. Wycliffe, a priest himself, initiated a reforming movement called Lollardry and struck out at worldly monks and bishops in sermons of terse power. In the Prologue Chaucer is frank, but good-humored, in his detestation of the fat Monk:

He was not pale as a fore-pined ghost.
A fat swan loved he best of any roast.

The Monk is worldly, sybaritic, cynical, but far from vulgar. He has "full many a dainty horse" in stable, and he openly despises the monastic principles of poverty, chastity, and hard work. St. Augustine, or Austin, believed in "swink," or dedicated labor. "Let," says the Monk, "Austin have his swink to him reserved." He is witty, and he is also learned. When he is called on for his story, he provides a fine definition of tragedy and proceeds to give brisk shapely examples of tragic lives. The irony is subtle enough. If tragedy may be defined as the fall of a man from a high estate, then the Monk is himself well qualified to provide a tragic example for some other taleteller. But, of course, he has no sense of *hubris,* or insolence in the face of heaven.

The Pardoner, too, is gently presented as a reprehensible example of ecclesiastical abuse. He comes along with indulgences "from Rome al hoot" and a satchelful of dubious saintly relics—chiefly "pigges bones." These indulgences were, of course, something over a century later to be the pretext for Luther's first battle with the Roman Church, a battle that was inflamed into the great war of the Reformation. In Chaucer's time the selling of grace, or of the remission of temporal punishment meted out by the Church for sin, was already a notorious scandal. And yet the Pardoner is a formidable and rather admirable figure. His invective against the sins of gluttony, drunkenness, gambling, and swearing is impressive, and his story is perhaps the best of the lot. It is a story that I have told to the least literary, even the least literate, of scholastic or social groups (on guard duty in the army, for instance), and I have never yet known it to fail to move its audience.

It is about three drunken revelers who resent the death of one of their friends during a period of plague. In their drunken state Death becomes personified as a tangible, though invisible, enemy; and they set out to find Death and kill him. An old man tells them that they will find Death under a particular tree, but what they discover there instead is a pile of gold. Each aims at getting the treasure for himself. Two of them mount guard over the treasure during the night, sending the third off to buy provisions. On his return, the other two at once kill him and get down to eating and drinking what he has brought. But the wine is poisoned. All three lie there under the tree with the useless gold, having found what they sought.

Chaucer contrasts the worldly hypocrisy of the Monk and the Pardoner with the Parson's Tale, which comes last. This parish priest is a good and pious man, self-denying, hard-working, totally unambitious, and the so-called tale he tells is a worthy sermon in prose, dealing with penitence, the diagnostics of sin, and the nature of sin's remedies. As we know, *The Canterbury Tales* was never completed, and it is conceivable that this platitudinous dissertation is the mere raw material that Chaucer proposed working up into a lively verse homily. But it is

MONK

much more likely that the poet is being conventionally pious and, belatedly, making up for the gross salaciousness of such stories as the Miller's and the Carpenter's. One fears that Chaucer was of the devil's party without knowing it. Certainly he never seems, with any conviction, to be on the side of the cenobitic virtues: he is all for the rich, sensuous, bawdy variety of the world.

ook, for instance, at the Wife of Bath's prologue to her own tale. The tale itself is not remarkable—an adaptation of Gower's story of Florent in his *Confessio Amantis*. It tells of a knight at King Arthur's court who, condemned to death for rape, is given a year to find the answer to the riddle "What is the thing that women most desire?" and thus escape execution. A foul old witch tells him she will give him the answer on condition that he marry her. He has to assent, whereupon she turns into a lovely young woman. The answer to the riddle is "Sovereignty." Before this unexceptional fable the Wife of Bath regales us with a lengthy and vigorous attack on celibacy. Man, she says, in her medieval way, was not given a penis merely to micturate, nor was woman endowed with the complementary organ for the same negative purpose. Sex is a great thing, and her own life has been a hymn to it. She has had five husbands and regretted none of them. Here are some of her own words, or rather J. U. Nicholson's modernization of them, about her marriage to her fifth:

To church my man was borne upon the morrow
By neighbours, who for him made signs of sorrow;
And Jenkin, our good clerk, was one of them.
So help me God, when rang the requiem
After the bier, I thought he had a pair
Of legs and feet so clean-cut and so fair
That all my heart I gave to him to hold.
He was, I think, but twenty winters old,
And I was forty, if I tell the truth;
But then I always had a young colt's tooth.
Gap-toothed I was, and that became me well;
I had the print of holy Venus' seal.
So help me God, I was a healthy one,
And fair and rich and young and full of fun;

SQUIRE

And truly, as my husbands all told me,
I had the silkiest *quoniam* that could be. . . .
Venus gave me my lust, my lickerishness,
And Mars gave me my sturdy hardiness . . .

The Wife of Bath is, in the modern phrase, all woman, and she stands forever as a warning to us not to regard all women of the past as prudish, ignorant, and downtrodden just because these were the desired attributes of Victorian woman. Read the Clerk's Tale, and no other of these, and it is easy enough to assume that medieval women were meek chattels. But in that tale of poor patient Griselda, whose fortitude, trust, and faith in the face of a virtue-testing husband make one grind one's teeth and almost shout to her to sock the loving sadist in his own, Chaucer is merely balancing the Wife of Bath's strong earthiness with a nightmare ideal such as a henpecked third or fourth husband might dream of—a dream not to be realized, of course. The game of Absolute Virtue, Unbreakable Virginity, or Unflinching Chivalric Courage was part of the culture of the fourteenth century, a kind of beguiling intellectual sport. Griselda is no more to be taken seriously than is the submissive Katharina at the end of *The Taming of the Shrew*. Women have never yet been tamed, except, apparently, during that mad, unclean widowhood at Windsor.

Of all these tales the most maddening is the Squire's (and what a wholesome unhippyish young man he is), because it is unfinished. There can be no doubt of the intervention of Chaucer's death: the story breaks off and the Squire promises a continuation that we do not get. If he was bored, it is hard to understand why, for this legend of the king of Arabia's gift of a magic ring to Canace, daughter of King Cambuscan of Tartary, through which she can understand the language of birds is—so far as it goes—enchanting. John Milton evidently thought so, for in *Il Penseroso* he dreamed he might

... call up him who left half told
The story of Cambuscan bold,
Of Camball and of Algarsife,
And who had Canace to wife.

If we want the rest of that story we have to wade through Spenser's *Faerie Queene,* which, though beautiful, is monotonous and decidedly un-Chaucerian.

The dullest of these pilgrims' stories is that told by Chaucer himself, characterized as timid and with a groundward look, and called upon to entertain the company in the following words by Harry Bailey:

Approche neer, and loke up merily.
Now war yow, sirs, and lat this man have place;
He in the waast is shape as wel as I;
This were a popet in an arm t'enbrace
For any womman, smal and fair of face.
He semeth elvish by his contenaunce,
For un-to no wigth dooth he daliaunce.

Sey now somwhat, sin other folk han sayd;
Tel us a tale of mirthe, and that anoon ...

But this absent-looking clerk, who has created all the pilgrims and all their tales, pleads his lack of skill in storytelling. When he is persuaded to try his hand, unhandy as he is, he embarks upon the story of Sir Thopas—a sly little satire on knight-errantry. The verse is decent but not exciting, and we are grateful when Harry Bailey breaks in to say that this will not do at all. Thereupon Chaucer tells, in prose as flat as long-opened soda water, the story of Melibeus, "a moral tale vertuous" translated from a French romance. Glumly we hear him to the end, and we must surmise that the other pilgrims also are glum though polite.

CLERK OF OXENFORD

This is a joke worthy of James Joyce —one of those dangerous expositions of deliberate dullness that only justify themselves through the willingness of the creator to push on dully to the limit. But this is English rather than Irish humor; it is the RAF pilot understating his heroism, the prime minister saying that a landslide election victory is a reasonably good show. The great poet denies even his competence. One can hardly imagine this kind of deliberate nonachievement coming from, say, a German or a French poet.

Had the whole vast scheme been completed, *The Canterbury Tales* would have rivaled *War and Peace* for length. But its unfinished state is also a peculiar virtue, bringing the work closer to life than to art, for though it is in the nature of a work of art to have a beginning and an end, life itself is a continuum. The Canterbury pilgrims never reach Canterbury; they are still on their way there. They have stories still to tell, but the telling must be deferred forever. We can never know who wins the prize and eats the free supper. To be forced to leave a work unfinished is to solve, involuntarily, a large artistic problem, for no writer yet has been satisfied with the way his book ends.

It is because *The Canterbury Tales* is a beguiling, a multiple and various, entertainment that the captious have been disposed to rate it low—lower than *Paradise Lost,* which seeks to justify the ways of God to man, or *Hamlet,* which is full of ontological and eschatological problems. In Chaucer's time there was no need for religious epic as self-justification, and there was no room for the deeper philosophical inquiries. The purpose of life was cut and dried—to survive on the plane of subsistence, to prepare for the next world. All the rest was time-filling—the waging of war, the games of taletelling, chess, and courtly love. After a long period in which man has accorded the leafiest palms to earnest writers, to writers crammed with meaning and

NUN'S PRIEST

message, we are all beginning to learn once more that art is not concerned with the transmission of separable meanings—moral precepts, philosophical systems—but with images of human life encapsulated in apparently irrelevant shapes. An age that gives Samuel Beckett the Nobel Prize, finding a desirable work of art in a play about two tramps who play word games while waiting for what will never come, should be ready to see much virtue in Chaucer.

He is one of the few writers of the Middle Ages who doesn't have to be coddled with that antiquarian reverence we give to names the common man has never had any desire to know —names like Langland, Henryson, Gower, the authors of *Pearl* and *The Owl and the Nightingale.* The eternal relevance of Chaucer may come clear when a film has been made of *The Canterbury Tales.* I suppose I must be one of many who have attempted screenplays, hoping for backers who never appear, based on those of the stories that lend themselves most obviously to the medium (*not* Sir Thopas, *not* patient Griselda). The Nun's Priest's Tale of the rooster and the fox is clearly animation material; the Pardoner's Tale is all stark visuality; the Knight's Tale is as rich as *Camelot.* It may be a long time before GEOFFREY CHAUCER appears on the credit list, but there is no hurry. After all, we've already waited nearly six hundred years.

Anthony Burgess, one of the most prolific writers of novels, short stories, and essays around, is spending the year as a visiting lecturer at Princeton. His most recent article for HORIZON, *on Burton's* Anatomy of Melancholy, *appeared last fall, just before publication (by Knopf) of his ambitious study,* Shakespeare.

ODD COUPLES

I was rather astonished when a minibus drove up to my house one day last summer and out poured ten children. They had with them two parents, but not one child had them both in common as mother and father, and two of the children belonged to neither parent, but to a former husband of a wife who had died. Both parents, well into middle age, had just embarked, he on his fourth, she on her third, marriage.

The children, who came in all sizes and ranged from blond Nordic to jet-haired Greek, bounced around the garden, as happy as any children I have ever seen. To them, as Californians, their situation did not seem particularly odd; most of their friends had multiple parents. Indeed, to them, the odd family may have been the one that Western culture has held up as a model for two thousand years or more—the lifelong union of a man and wife. It took me a long time to believe that these children could be either happy or well adjusted. And yet, are they a sign of the future, of the way the world is going?

Unlike anthropologists or sociologists, historians have not studied family life closely. Until recently, we knew very little about the age at which people married in western Europe before the nineteenth century, or about how many children they had, or what the rate of illegitimacy might be, or whether, when newly wed, they lived with their parents or set up a home of their own.

Few of these questions can be answered with exactitude even now, but we can make better guesses. We still know little about the sexual practices that marriage covered, a subject to which historians are only just turning their attention. But we do know much more about the function of family life —its social role—particularly if we turn from the centuries to the millenniums and pay attention to the broad similarities rather than to the fascinating differences between one region and another. If we do this, we realize that the family has changed far more profoundly than even that busload of Californians might lead us to expect.

Basically, the family has fulfilled three social functions—it has provided a labor force, transmitted property, and educated and trained children, not only into accepted social patterns, but also in the work skills upon which their future subsistence depended. Until very recent times, the vast majority of children never went to school at all; their school was the family, where they learned to dig and sow and reap and herd their animals, or learned their father's craft of smith or carpenter or potter. The unitary family was particularly good at coping with the small peasant holdings that covered most of the world's fertile regions from China to Peru. In the primitive peasant world a child of five or six could begin to earn his keep in the fields, as he still can in India and Africa.

It was the primitive nature of the peasant economy that gave the family its wide diffusion and its remarkable continuity. To what extent the family existed before the Neolithic revolution we shall never know, but certainly it gained in strength as men became rooted to the soil. Many primitive peoples, hunters and food gatherers, who live today in preagrarian societies tend to have a looser structure of marriage, and the women a far greater freedom of choice and easier divorce, than is permitted in peasant societies.

There can be little doubt that the Neolithic revolution created new opportunities for the family, partly because this revolution created new property relations. But more important, it created great masses of property, beyond anything earlier societies had known.

After the revolution in agriculture, property and its transmission lay at the very heart of social relations and possessed an actuality that we find hard to grasp. Although we are much richer, possessions are now more anonymous —often little more than marks in a ledger—and what we own constantly changes. But for the majority of mankind over the past seven thousand

The traditional family was a landholding economic unit, like these Nebraska farmers of the 1890's.

years property has been deeply personal and familial—a plot of land, a house, or perhaps no more than the tools and materials of a craft. Yet these possessions were keys both to survival and to betterment. Hence they were endowed with magic power, bound up with the deepest roots of personality.

In all societies the question of property became embedded in almost every aspect of family life, particularly marriage and the hereditary rights of children. Because of property's great importance, subservience of women and children to the will of the father, limited only by social custom, became the pattern of most peasant societies. Marriage was sanctified not only by the rites of religion but by the transmission of property. Few societies could tolerate freedom of choice in marriage—too much vital to the success or failure of a family depended on it: an ugly girl with five cows was a far fairer prospect than a pretty girl with one.

And because of the sexual drives of frail human nature, the customs of marriage and of family relationships needed to be rigorously enforced. Some societies reversed the sexually restrictive nature of permanent marriage and permitted additional wives, but such permission was meaningless to the poverty-stricken mass of the peasantry. And, as we shall see, the patterns of family life were always looser for the rich and the favored.

But a family was more than property expressed in real goods; it was for thousands of years both a school and a tribunal: the basic unit of social organization whose function in modern society has been largely taken over by the state. In most peasant societies life was regulated by the village community, by the patriarchs of the village, and the only officer of the central government that these villagers saw with any regularity was the taxgatherer. As societies grew more complex—and this is true particularly of the West during the past four hundred years—life became regulated by the nation-state or by the growth in power and importance of

As the tight family structure rooted to the soil breaks down, a new, more fluid one replaces it. None of the Richard Burtons' children is the issue of their own marriage.

more generalized local communities—the town or county.

This has naturally weakened the authority of heads of families, which changes in social custom symbolically illustrate. No child in western Europe would have dared to sit unbidden in the presence of his parents before the eighteenth century; if he had, he would surely have been punished. No head of a household would have thought twice about beating a recalcitrant young servant or apprentice before the end of the nineteenth century. For a younger brother to marry without the consent of the eldest brother would have been regarded as a social enormity, and sisters were disposable property.

All of this power has vanished. Indeed, we find it hard to grasp the intensity of family relationships of other times or their complexity, so rapidly have family ties disintegrated in the past hundred years. Today nearly all children in the Western world are educated outside the home from about the age of five. The skills they learn are rarely transmitted by their parents, and they learn about the nature of their own world, about its social structure, outside the family.

Although the economic and educational functions of the family have declined, many of us still feel that it provides the most satisfactory emotional basis for human beings; that a secure

family life breeds stability and a capacity not only for happiness but for adjusting to society's demands. This, too, may be based on misjudgment, since family life in the past was not remarkable for its happiness. We get few glimpses into the private lives of men and women long dead, but when we do, we often find strain, frustration, and petty tyranny. For so many human beings family life was a prison from which there was no escape.

The family as the basic social group first began to fail, except in its property relations, among the aristocracy. The majority of the affluent of western Europe have always created for themselves a double standard, particularly as far as sex is concerned. In a few cities, such as Calvin's Geneva, the purity of family life might be maintained, but the aristocracies of France, Italy, and Britain tolerated, without undue concern, adultery, homosexuality, and the sexual freedom that, for better or worse, we consider the hallmark of modern life.

But what we think of as the social crises of this generation—the rapid growth of divorce, the emancipation of women and adolescents, the sexual and educational revolutions; all the things that are steadily making the family weaker and weaker—are the inexorable result of the changes in society itself. The family as a unit of social organization was remarkably appropriate for a less complex world of agriculture and craftsmanship, but ever since industry and highly urbanized societies began to replace that world, the social functions of the family have steadily weakened. It is a process not likely to be halted.

There is no historical reason to believe that human beings would be less or more happy, less or more stable, as a result. Like every human institution, the family has been molded by the changing needs of society, sometimes slowly, sometimes quickly. And that busload of children does no more than symbolize the failure, not of marriage, but of the role of the old-fashioned family unit in a modern, urbanized, scientific, and affluent society.

Arabic Aden, a seaport controlled at different times by Romans, Turks, Englishmen, and Yemenites, is built in the crater of an extinc

SHELTER
FOR
A DARK AGE

When cities were in turmoil
and brigands loose in the land, a man's home was,
of necessity, his castle

By BERNARD RUDOFSKY

For all one knows there will always be an Englishman who refers to his home as his castle. The conceit persists unchallenged because the castle in question is fictitious. A gulf of roughly ten centuries separates modern man from the time when castles were a common commodity, indeed a necessity. Apart from ruins, what passes for castles today are the products of architectural taxidermy—mummified mansions, national monuments, and occasionally, houses of royalty (itself a species on the brink of extinction).

Castles, the strong metaphor of man's presumed self-sufficiency, are an

volcano. Castles cling like barnacles to the surrounding mountains in this view from Georg Braun's Civitates Orbis Terrarum *of 1581.*

Old World institution; the combination of residence and fortress occurs mainly in Europe, Asia, and Africa. Although Americans are not averse to anachronisms and have produced their quota of pseudo-medieval churches and colleges, they seem to draw the line at castles. Castles are as un-American as a mistress; the man who has everything collects credit cards, not castles. To him a castle is not a house or a home but the moldy container of the darkest aspects of the Dark Ages. Incapacitated for feelings of grandeur by his upbringing, he has as much difficulty imagining himself living in feudal surroundings as wearing armor to his office. To come across an inhabited medieval castle is as much of a shock to him as hearing a museum's dinosaur neigh. Like quills and snuffers, medieval castles are considered obsolete. They are the fossils of architecture, an uncomfortable reminder of a time when wars were still fought with arrows and lances, when killing was a handicraft rather than an industry. No architect within living memory has been commissioned to build a castle, and I don't mean a château. West Point, Alcatraz, and San Simeon—all of them brave attempts to graft heroic silhouettes onto the landscape—received no plaudits. Neither did urban armories or those now-defunct town houses optimistically referred to as châteaux. The word "château" is the same as *castillo,* but the stiletto-sharp syllables of the latter have been blunted and the *s* has given way to the broad circumflex accent. The château lacks the grimness of its Castilian counterpart; popular belief relegates the château to flat country, along lakes and rivers.

Today, when we are trying to rediscover the forgotten ties between architecture and the natural environment, we ought to take a good look at castles, those pivotal points in the landscape. Topographical accents par excellence, they are always commensurate to nature's scale. In particular, that loftiest place of abode, the crisp, rock-bound castle, recommends itself to our attention. An excrescence of the rocks, it perches on a hill or mountain in acrobatic suspense. It borrows its protective coloration from the environment in much the same way that a practiced Japanese "steals" the trees' silhouettes of his neighbor's garden. It is all stone; no leprous stucco, no peeling paint. The feudal touch is usually provided by an eye-catching cliff, a mesa, or a dense forest, all of them anathema to the democratically-minded builder. Wherever modern man puts up a building—in the country or in a town—he is bent on annihilating its natural setting. Any outcrop—a tree, a boulder—must be pulverized so that he can better visualize his creation. He is a leveler at heart. For his flight of thought he needs, as it were, an airstrip, an expanse of nothing.

In the beginning a castle was just an earth mound, surrounded by a dry ditch. The mound's crest may have carried a palisade no more protective than the one the Pilgrims erected around Plimoth Town. Indeed, about the year 1000 the art of building defenses in Europe had not developed beyond the know-how the Assyrians brought to constructing the walls and towers of Nineveh. It was only during the Crusades—a span of almost two centuries—that the incombustible castle emerged. Out of this unspeakably hideous chapter of history came a better understanding of architecture in general, and of fortifications in particular. Discounting treachery, a castle built on high ground often remained impregnable; that is, until gunpowder came into use. It was perhaps the only time when a walled-in and well-provisioned populace was justified in experiencing a feeling of absolute security in the face of an invader.

But life was not thought worth living in a castle that was never assailed by forces stronger than the elements. Only during a siege did its true merits come to the fore. The battlements afforded a grand view of men locked in gladiatorial combat—a Colosseum turned inside out, with the grandstand in the center and the stage in the round. Even when the attackers succeeded in breaching a wall, little was lost. The defenders just hopped from one perch to another, dousing assailants with pitch and molten lead, missiles as deadly as bullets. A siege in full swing pinpointed the im-

This woodcut from the Schwäbische Chronik, *1486, depicts the siege of what looks like an impregnable castle. Judged by modern artillery standards, the arquebus's impact would seem to equal that of a woodpecker.*

perfections in layout and structure, and the burgrave would make a mental note to have the level of the moat—a castle's Plimsoll line—slightly raised, or to make the hard-edge towers round. Castles so strong that their bastions were never put to the test remained inviolate until wreckers began to quarry them for building materials.

To ferret out early castle architecture in its natural habitat one must go to Spain, where one is rarely out of sight of castles or their ruins. The northern highland, peppered with peels and keeps, is known as Castile, the name being derived from *castillos,* the frontier defenses that guarded the country against the Moors. (Similarly, Austria's easternmost province is called Burgenland, literally, castle country.) Today, when the sites of a good many castles have been "developed," "landscaped," or otherwise defaced, one must seek the true aerie to which no road, no path, ascends. Usually, it is partly in ruins, superbly aged, bathed

The wooden castles of Scandinavia introduced a light note into the architecture of fortifications. This 1502 drawing shows Älvsborg, then a bone of contention between Sweden and Denmark.

by the rains and swept by the winds, the self-appointed curators of castle architecture. The aesthetic pedant who alights on a castle pitched high on a mountaintop is dismayed by what he takes to be its unruliness. Its very substance proves to be elusive because it seldom permits one to optically grasp its exact shape. One simply cannot walk around it; an inspection of its circumference might lead to a broken neck.

There are compensations. Only up there does one get the perfect bird-of-prey's-eye view of a world by now as remote as the stars—a scented landscape covered with groves of gnarled olive trees whose trunks resemble Chinese ideographs; a modest river, icebound in winter, swollen in spring, dry in summer, when veritable oleander woods emblazon the stony bed; a narrow lane, a cloud of dust kicked up by an ambulant herd of sheep; a camel-back bridge, a walled cemetery, and low in the castle's shade, a village of whitewashed houses.

Orthodox architectural history deals for the most part with buildings that have served mankind as physical and spiritual first-aid stations—temples, cathedrals, theatres, and thermae—to the exclusion of permanent habitations. No doubt the towering castle is somewhat unwieldy, too intricate to be reduced to plans and façades. Yet castle anatomy is fairly simple. Although no two castles are quite alike, they can be broken down into a few basic patterns. In the publications of the International Castle Research Institute the castellologist Count de Caboga defined three "genuine" types: the square plan, which he calls the Arabic-Byzantine type; the Ringburg, or round, plan; and the irregularly shaped castle, which closely follows the terrain. Nearly all are built on the principle of the enclosed courtyard, the noble feature of the han, caravanserai, and Roman villa. The bulk of the buildings usually consists of the precise geometrical volumes—cubes, cylinders, cones, and

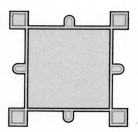

A good example of the square plan is represented by Montealegre Castle in Old Castile, Spain, at right and in the diagram above.

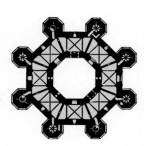

The two-story Castel del Monte in Apulia, Italy, right, typifies the round plan. Built about 1240 to the specifications of the Hohenstaufen emperor Frederick II as a hunting lodge, it alternately served as a residence and a state prison. Designed in Gothic style, it nevertheless presaged Renaissance architecture. Octagonal in plan, with eight towers for staircases, each floor contained eight marble-covered halls (see floor plan above). In its classical simplicity and crystalline precision it was the opposite of Nordic castles, with their turbid moats, gloomy courtyards, and their pell-mell mongrel architecture.

Sotalba Castle, right, on a mountaintop near Avila, Spain, represents an extreme case of the irregular plan. Stone walls insert themselves among gigantic boulders and natural bastions, creating an architectural mimicry.

Entrevaux, an ancient walled town in the French Maritime Alps, guards the access to several mountain passes. The castle is reached by a steep path that doubtless was a Calvary for assailants.

their subtle modulations—so close to the vision of early twentieth-century architects, the will-o'-the-wisp called functionalism. No balconies or stony curlicues detract from the overall tidiness. (Crenelations, we must remember, are not ornaments; every tooth hid a man intent on pouring death onto the assailant below.)

Taking into account the enormous diffusion of castles in former times—medieval Germany alone possessed more than ten thousand of them—the vast number of their inhabitants, and the fact that a country's population amounted to about one-tenth of what it is today, castles ranked high as dwelling places. Indeed, it would be a mistake to see them as purely military installations. They belong more nearly in the category of civilian shelter that in wartime gave refuge to peripheral folk, villagers, peasants, even burghers of neighboring towns. These emergency uses have been all but forgotten; the picture of the castle that takes hold of our imagination in childhood is that of an architectural toy tenanted by a fairy-tale prince with the looks of a page boy: an insipid creature, a youth, not a man. Not even in the hirsute era of Freud and Marx would he wear as much as a mustache. He never burned down villages or tortured his enemies. He did not give battle except when slaying dragons holding decorous, latter-day Andromedas in their clutches.

The bona fide knight was on intimate terms with the supernatural because his lair seemed to exert a special attraction for spirits, good and evil. But then, the earth was still flat, the heavens were hanging low, and divine intervention was more frequent than in our day. Saints still took a personal interest in people, and so did angels; to assist their charges, guardian angels would dive from a rift in the clouds to a faultless landing on a castle's battlements. Moreover, every castle had one or more resident ghosts as a matter of course, and was regularly visited by devils and demons. Best known in this respect is the Wartburg in Thuringia, the scene of the devil's encounter with Luther, who, displeased with his visitor, threw his inkpot at him. The ink was of the best quality, for the spot it left can still be seen.

A short etymological note on knighthood is perhaps in order. Originally the term "knight" applied to a person of modest station in life; the Old English *cniht*—*Knecht* in German—signified lowly helper. Romance languages, forever more polite and to the point, stress his superior means of transportation. The words "chevalier," *"caballero," "cavaliere,"* clearly refer to his equestrian status. The ravages of time have eroded this meaning; in today's Spain every man is a *caballero,* as a glance at toilet doors will confirm.

Some of the more exalted knights have been transmogrified into demigods inhabiting Valhalla-like castles whose dimensions remain unsurpassed by modern engineering. The classical example that helped to make mythomania so attractive is Arthur's Camelot. Thanks to Broadway and Hollywood, Artus de Bretagne is as familiar to our generation as Batman. In fact, some heroes of the medieval epic poems

This 1589 engraving by Daniel Specklin, author of a book on fortifications, immortalizes the Alsatian Fleckenstein Castle, which sat on a rock "cut like a diamond." It was razed in the seventeenth century.

So thick are the walls of Spain's Belmonte Castle that window sills become chambers. The opening has sprouted into a stone arbor.

behave quite like comic-strip characters. In the *Chanson de Roland* four knights kill four thousand Saracens; Roland himself continues fighting with his head split open. Yet King Arthur (who was not a king but a general) becomes more elusive the deeper one gets entangled with the particulars of his household. Just take a sober look at the magical Round Table.

It seems that in olden times problems of precedence were as pressing as they are today. For lack of a proper protocol Arthur's knights, an intensely sociable set—although, like French gourmets, they admitted no women at table—were forever at each other's throats to advance their standing, or more accurately, their seating. To put an end to their quarreling, tells Layamon, the thirteenth-century poet, a carpenter built a portable round table that seated sixteen hundred men. (There is no reason to think the poet was inventing it, we are assured by the *Encyclopaedia Britannica.*) Now, Ramsay and Sleeper's *Architectural Graphic Standards,* the modern builder's book of etiquette, allots to each person 2′ 0″ for comfortable seating. Unless the

knights sat in one another's laps like stacking chairs, the table's diameter came to more than one thousand feet, leaving several acres of waste space in the middle. No known castle hall, nor, for that matter, any present-day structure, could accommodate such an outsize piece of furniture.

The *historical* knight appears less mysterious. Not overexigent when it came to life's necessities, he was, however, avid of certain pleasures, such as hunting man and beast. Masculine to a fault, he was brimming with fighting spirit and, like the udder of the lost mountain goat, itching to be relieved of it. He possessed courage in excess of loyalty; indeed, he was implacably mercenary. El Cid, Spain's greatest hero, thought nothing of switching sides, free-lancing for Christians and Moors alike. It seems that a knight was bound only loosely by the code of his profession, if profession one could call it. He was probably far more practical than one might suppose, hard-fisted and stiff-necked, if only by virtue of his shiny battle outfit.

Knights are the Crustacea of the human species. Their workaday clothes may have been rustic, if not altogether tawdry, but their formal suit was not. A coat of mail was an extension of the castle, much as a car is an extension of the house. Like a car, it needed greasing and polishing and the smoothing of dents incurred in collisions and accidents. The services of a first-rate armorer were a knight's best life insurance and a boost to his *amour-propre*. Any red-nosed, grizzly-bearded knight clapped into his portable fortress was the picture of perfection. For armor is far more symmetrical than the man it encloses. Although stylized, it is a good counterfeit of the human form down to the tiniest bumps: the pigeony chest, coquettish waist, knuckles and finger tips, slitted eyes in a reptilian face (no Mongolism, merely a defensive squint), flaring nostrils but no metal ears. Although knights, when fighting one another, clashed like cymbals, they probably could not hear their own battle music. Nevertheless, armor was the thing; the men merely provided the stuffing, a sort of inner tube. Since armor is extremely rigid and far more body-building than a backboard, it must have been difficult to ascertain in the heat of a skirmish whether a galloping knight, solidly anchored in his stirrups and propped up by his scaffolding, was in control of his faculties, or badly wounded, or stone-dead. An unhinged, *fallen* knight was worth several times his weight in scrap metal. Patched and hammered into a second-

Among the merciless adversaries of a knight in full armor was the sun, which unavoidably turned his steely suit into a broiler. The clumsy umbrella, introduced in Renaissance days, not only marred his martial appearance but badly impaired his mobility. The 1548 drawing is from a tailor's manual in the Biblioteca Querini Stampalia in Venice.

hand suit, his armor would serve yet another knight or knave.

There was armor for boys, though not for women; belligerent amazons had no place in knightly society. (Jeanne d'Arc, who paid with her life for usurping male privileges, was never made a knight. This honor was reserved for her nineteenth-century compatriots Mme Curie and Rosa Bonheur, the

latter a devoted painter of horses.) Not that medieval woman was kept in monastic seclusion. The life of a castle's mistress, circa 1500, was filled with exercise and outdoor sports. As described in an old chronicle, her daily schedule began with prayers in the nearby woods, where early in the morning she went with her lady companions. They all brought their Books of Hours and devoutly refrained from talking. Next they heard mass in the castle's chapel and breakfasted on such dainties as roasted larks. Then the lady and her damsels joined the menfolk for a ride and amused themselves with forming sprays and sprigs into kinds of hats for their beaux, or listening to lays and ballads sung in polyphonic union. After a ceremonious banquet in the castle hall an entire hour was dedicated to dancing. Then followed a well-earned siesta to gather strength for another cavalcade, for frolicking and gamboling. Or, addressing herself to more serious matters, the chatelaine would indulge in some hunting, particularly the aristocratic pastime of falconry. In due time a picnic lunch was served, and after some more flower gathering and mutual festooning, the hunting party would repair to the castle for supper. The evening was concluded with digestive promenades and ball games and, the *pièce de résistance,* one more hour of dancing. A light snack and a nightcap brought the day to an end. Such, says the chronicler, was the daily routine.

No menus are extant from Arthur's time. We have, however, a detailed account of the food served (centuries later, in 1578) on the occasion of Wilhelm von Rosenberg's wedding at Krummenau in Bohemia, now Český Krumlov. Among the ingredients of the meal, or meals, are listed 370 oxen, 113 stags, 98 wild boars, 2,292 hares, 3,910 partridges, 22,687 thrushes, 12,-887 chickens, and 3,000 capons. These meaty viands were balanced by proportional amounts of eel, pike, carp, and salmon, and 5 tons of oysters; 40,-

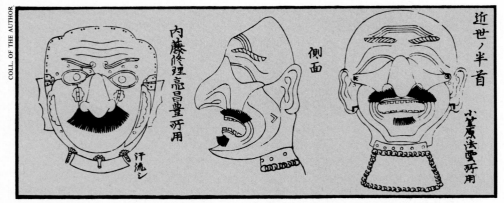

The armorer's art had its humorous touches. These delicately hinged false faces, with wrinkles, raised brows, and thick mustaches, are from a seventeenth-century Japanese reference book.

Venus rather than Mars reigns over the everyday life of knightly society. Baccio Baldini's 1460 engraving records the amorous goings on in a bucolic setting protected by five castles, four of which appear on the horizon.

837 eggs were broken, 6,405 pails of wine dispensed to maintain appetite and promote digestion. Pantries resembled city markets; kitchens took on the aspect of blast furnaces.

Nor was the entertainment accompanying the meal of the puny kind we are used to today. Instead of somniferous luncheon speeches, meals were served to the dulcet sounds of flute and shawm. There were mock combats, riding and dancing exhibitions, fireworks, and mummeries. At Rosenberg's wedding a touch of circus was provided by monkeys riding on goatback while playing the harp, a feat that Hollywood could not duplicate for money or good words.

Of course, such gorgeous fare was the exception; poor knights often had to make do with potluck and listen to the high winds plucking chords from the fir trees. In the noblest castles the protein diet consisted of crows, cranes, ravens, storks, swans, and even vultures, each and all muscular birds. In anti-culinary England meals were usually of the beggarly kind: salted fish, tough legumes, and indigestible des-

A brush drawing done in 1788 by Nanko Haruki shows Hameji Castle. The tallest and most massive of Japan's ancient buildings, at one time it was crowned with thirty turrets. The magnificent five-story donjon, or main tower, sits in splendor upon a stone wall that is eighty feet high.

This is the high-ceilinged breakfast room of the Parador del Emperador at Fuenterrabia, a former castle of Emperor Charles V. The castle dates in part from the twelfth century.

serts were the order of the day. The entire cooking for the week was done on Sunday and warmed up at 10 A.M. for lunch and at the ungodly hour of 4 P.M. for dinner.

The idea of what is desirable is not innate or unalterable, and it would be unjust to gauge the former amenities of castles by our own scale of values. People who get lyrical about twelve-foot ceilings in brownstone houses might find breakfasting in a six-story-high baronial hall a transporting experience (available today at small expense in those castles that have been converted into hostelries). Most of us, though, have never developed a taste for spaciousness, cooped up in mini-apartments as we are most of the time. Another insight into knightly luxury is afforded by the descriptions of their beds. Some were of heroic size, and if the mattresses did not always correspond to our ideas of molluscan

comfort, the bedspreads were sometimes precious beyond our commercially conditioned imagination. What modern housewife could conceive of bedcovers made of ermine and black sable or of veritable Oriental tents for canopies? The Styrian minnesinger Ulrich von Lichtenstein described his ladylove's voluptuous bed as conscientiously as a modern home-furnishings editor. Her velvet mattress was covered by two silk sheets, a comforter, and blissful (*"wunniglich"*) cushions, while carpets served for a canopy. At the foot of the bed stood two candelabra, and the walls of the room "were hung with a hundred lights."

The flowering of castles produced some exotic blooms in Japan, where the art of fortifications was, if not introduced, at least greatly improved by, of all people, European missionaries. Like Japanese armor, Japanese castles have a flavor all their own. The cyclopean *curved* walls that rise from the moat, of an elegance unknown in the Western world, form a strange contrast to the highly flammable wooden structures inside. For sheer size, no other nation can match their building stones; the largest of them, used in the construction of Osaka Castle, is 19' 2" high and 47' 6" long, or about the width of two brownstone houses and the height of two floors. The keep always surprises by its exquisite carpentry and downright homelike atmosphere. Above all, it is as spotless as an old-fashioned inn. Naturally, one has to take off one's shoes before entering it, a ritual that cannot but have had a pacifying effect on the most sanguinary of soldiers. Can anybody imagine an American general leaving his shoes in front of the Pentagon?

About a century ago, when the Japanese embraced Western-style progressiveness and in the course of a few years appropriated Western conventions of warfare, the sight of their outmoded castles made them uncomfortably aware of their backwardness. Not being overattached to their past, they simply de-

Elegantly curved cyclopean masonry forms a solid base for the flammable wood structures of Japanese castles. Kumamoto's walls are designated Important Cultural Property.

cided to do away with their castles. They leveled the bastions and filled the moats and publicly auctioned off the assorted architecture. A turret went for the equivalent of three American dollars, a donjon for ten, while the wooden structures of an entire castle, sold for fuel, brought the sum of seventy-five dollars. Castles that remained standing because they found no ready buyers were incinerated in the air raids of World War II.

Since then the Japanese have had second thoughts about their feudal architecture. Twenty years ago the reconstruction of Osaka Castle sparked off a castle boom that is long in subsiding. What patriotism destroyed is now being re-created, thanks to commercial tourism. Chambers of commerce are rivaling historical societies in resurrecting the past, and castles are rising from the ashes in their old splendor with not a few innovations. Thus, the woodwork now is hung from steel and reinforced concrete frames, and elevators comfort the lame and footsore. Today, Japanese castles are built as tourist attractions, and by no means for foreigners only, in places where there had never been a castle before.

In Europe some castles have been undergoing similar rehabilitation. They are rarely put up for sale, but they have a collector's value, the collectors being not individuals but well-endowed institutions or the state. Since 1926 the Spanish government has been turning castles slowly but persistently into stateowned hotels. This is by no means a newfangled idea; when chivalry ceased to rule the world, and knighthood dissolved in the acid test of time, a number of nobles took up the lucrative business of catering to the lowborn. They never parted with the insignia of their former status, and preserved intact their coats of arms in the form of signboards. All those White Horses, Black Eagles, and Red Lions one encounters so frequently in central Europe hint at the innkeepers' noble ancestry. Even more explicit are the names of Span-

The photographs in this column show three views of the Castillo de Santa Catalina at Jaén, Spain, a luxuriously appointed inn.

Elaborately sculptured coats of arms flank the parador's *main entrance, much like our recommendatory shingles of travel clubs.*

Although Jaén's parador *contains only seven guest rooms, the lobby (above) is sumptuous and the dining hall seats two hundred. People are dwarfed by the cathedral-sized spaces.*

71

Cena
Medieval
Mozárabe

★

El Ajo Blanco de Almendras
★
La Pipirrana
★
Las Habas fritas con Huevo
★
El Cordero Asado
★
La Ensalada
★
Los Alfajores Blancos y Negros
Las Yemas de Santa Ursula
El Tocino del Cielo de Ubeda
Las Torrijas
El Pastel de Dátil
El Pastel de Guarromán
★
El Moka Arabe
★
Vinos Aloque y De la Torre

Stylish Mozarabic suppers are served with all the complications of a long-vanished table etiquette at the castle inn of Santa Catalina at Jaén. The meal is composed to suit a contemporary stomach: roast lamb is preceded by garlicky appetizers, cured ham, and beans fried with eggs. Vegetables are not much in evidence; desserts consist of tarts, gingerbread, and unholy concoctions of sugar, bacon, egg yolks, dates, honey, and flour.

ish medieval castle inns: Parador del Emperador, de la Emperatriz, de los Reyes Católicos. The names are legitimate. At Jarandilla, for instance, guests are put up in the quarters where Emperor Charles V, one of the most powerful monarchs of all time, not merely slept but spent some time in retirement shortly before his death. For a nominal fee one has the run of palatial premises that no American hostelry can match. Stony edifices with walls from three to ten feet thick are honeycombed with apartments, a paradoxical combination of vastness and downright Oriental economy of space. Each room

is different in shape and size, differently furnished and decorated. (The coffered or painted ceiling is somewhat out of reach, but may be studied with the aid of binoculars.) Labyrinthine corridors and staircases lead to arcaded courtyards, patios and cool promenades, gardens complete with arbors and fountains, a chapel, a belvedere, and many semisecret nooks tucked away in towers and battlements.

Alas, the paradorial food is disappointing. One scrutinizes the menu in vain for wild boar, for peacock or like heraldic birds; the fare is mercilessly up-to-date. Lately, though, great efforts have been made at elevating the sights of the sandwich–and–ice-cream–conditioned tourist by staging "medieval suppers" at a number of castle inns. With drums beating and trumpets sounding, boards that groan under the load of food, or so it seems, are carried by pages in stately procession to the refectory. The table setting is discreetly backdated with the help of porringers, tankards and goblets, wine jars, and water pitchers for washing one's hands. To keep the gastric juices flowing, a perambulating troubadour sings of bold men's bloody combatings

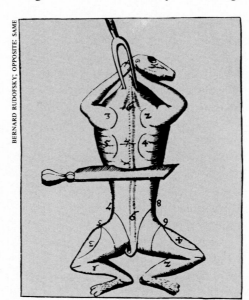

BERNARD RUDOFSKY; OPPOSITE: SAME

A sanguinary touch, provided at gastronomic festivities, was the display and subsequent dismembering of succulent corpses. The diagram is from a manual on the art of carving.

At Almansa, in the province of Albacete, a majestic fortress of Arabic origin (opposite) rises above the town, guarding what was once the principal gate to the interior of Spain.

and gentle ladies' tears, and of a feudal age's main preoccupation, the wars against the infidels. The dishes are worth a detour if only for their unfamiliarity: *Sopa Boba,* "crazy soup," mentioned in *Don Quixote,* a broth made from gizzards and pounded almonds; *La Merced de Dio,* "God's mercy," or eggs fried in honey, which the nuns used to serve visiting worthies; and so on.

The discriminating eater, however, will do well to cross the border. Portugal counts among its *pousadas* a few reconstituted castles whose kitchens are singularly capable of pleasing one's palate; the parade of hors d'oeuvres alone has all the gaiety of a minor folk festival. However, the country that might triumph in a national contest to revive the medieval pleasures of the table is France. The very word "château" suggests rich food and vintage wines. A *château aux pommes frites*— short for Châteaubriand—or a bottle of *Château Margaux,* is, every bite and drop, artistically on a level with the creations of, say, Viollet-le-Duc, the supreme restaurateur and confectioner of medieval architecture. Recently, France has indicated an interest in following the Iberian example of castle redemption. If the project comes off, travel will be greatly enriched, caloriewise. The French might very well rise to the occasion and write a new chapter in castellology, a cookbook of medieval culinary art, to fill with tantalizing odors a species of architecture unjustly considered passé.

Bernard Rudofsky has written for Horizon *on other architectural subjects: covered streets, cave dwellings, and roads. His next book will deal with what might be called body architecture: the clothes, make-up, and disguises men and women use to "improve on" nature.*

THE
ASHANTI

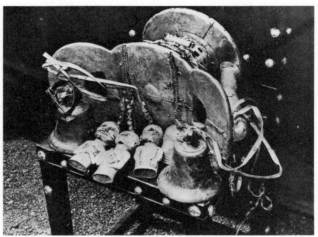

The Golden Stool, upon which no one may sit, is believed by the Ashanti to be the divine source of royal authority. Left, a tribesman stands guard during the coronation of a new king.

Remarkable artists and proud rulers
of the African rain forest, they were humbled
in the last century by British
colonial invaders. Yet the spirit of their nation
lives on, embodied in a
strange and hidden talisman: the Golden Stool

By JAMES MORRIS

Festooned with fetishes and animal tails, an Ashanti warrior, right, wears full regalia in an English engraving of 1819. His weapons include a small spear, a bow strapped to his back, and a quiver of poisoned arrows tied to his wrist. During this period Ashanti troops had also begun to fight with muskets.

Near the beginning of the eighteenth century, Okomfo Anokye, fetish priest to Osei Tutu the Asantahene, received from Heaven the Golden Stool of Friday: a token, a repository, a mysterious gold-encrusted throne hung as the centuries passed with talismanic emblems—golden handcuffs, human masks, bells, thongs, images—never to be used as a seat or even allowed to touch the ground, but to be cherished forever as the dwelling place of the *sunsum,* or spirit of a nation. So, in legend, was created the sacred empire of the Ashanti, one of the most remarkable of the lost powers of Africa, whose sense of nationhood survives to this day and whose fatal confrontation with the forces of the Christian West affords a sad insight into the impulses of history.

The country of the Ashanti forms the forested interior of what is now Ghana. It is archetypal West Africa—largely rain forest, hot, damp, steamy, thick with luxuriant, tangled foliage, well populated with villages of mud, thatch, and corrugated iron, whose people seem to live lives of theatrical bonhomie. They are a volatile people, quick to courtesy or anger, dressed for the most part in the dazzlingly colored *kente* cloth of their tradition; and they possess a culture of such ancient and poetic complexity that to most Western

visitors it must remain an unapproachable enigma. It is this elusive quality of their pride, set against the boisterous gaudiness of their daily lives, that gives poignancy to the story of their relations with the West.

For these were armies that clashed in ignorance, like Arnold's armies of the night. Neither side remotely understood the other. The Ashanti pagan culture on the one hand, the European Christian civilization on the other, were movements of immense aggressive assurance, armored in religious faith. If it looks to us in hindsight like an unequal conflict, between European imperialism in its heyday and an unlettered kingdom of the bush, it did not seem so imbalanced at the time: while the Western generals had their Gatling guns and their rocket batteries, the king of Ashanti went into battle hung all over, head to foot, with infallible jujus—forming a kind of spiritual chain mail—fastened so thickly to his person that his face scarcely showed through the magical fragments. When he moved, the whole silhouette of his presence menacingly rippled.

When I was recently in Kumasi, the capital of the Ashanti nation, I visited the mausoleum of the Ashanti kings, a crumbled structure, which stands beside a busy main thoroughfare. Its iron gates were unlocked, and as I pushed them a gardener approached

me, strangely smiling, and bowed me a welcome. He looked a little mad, I thought, bowing and grinning at me, but I returned his greeting and opened the gate. Instantly a bloodcurdling cry sounded behind my back. There stood, vermilion *kente* cloth slung across his shoulders, the most ferociously alarming old man I have ever seen. His face was furiously contorted. Screaming importunities at me, he drew his finger luridly across his throat and violently gestured at me to keep out. I hesitated, looking from one man to the other, the fulsomely bowing idiot, the frenzied elder; and as I did so the little crowd that had gathered on the pavement shouted its urgent advice: "Don't go! Keep out! You'll never come out again! Go home!"

I went, realizing that my solecism was far more than social, and I later discovered the sanctity of the mausoleum to be so utter that even great men of the royal household, after forty years in the service of the monarchy, had never set foot inside it.

This terrible holiness of authority always distinguished Ashanti society, and it was one of the prime causes of Ashanti success. Until Osei Tutu's time the Ashanti were merely one constituent tribe of the Akan group of peoples, who probably came to the Gold Coast out of the north sometime during the Middle Ages. Their original home was

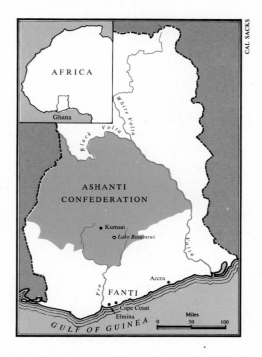

The Ashanti Confederation, shown in green, once included about one-third of the area of present-day Ghana, the former colony of the Gold Coast. Center for British forays against the Ashanti was Cape Coast, a European town set in the midst of the Ashanti's most formidable native rivals, the Fanti.

the country around Lake Bosumtwi, a gloomy tree-fringed mere that intermittently belches gas and mud from its recesses and is thought by some Africans to be the hole out of which their ancestors first crawled. It was during the seventeenth century that the Ashanti entered history. They immediately began to display a talent for organization, both civic and military, altogether exceptional among West African peoples. Gradually they constructed a confederation of Akan tribes whose separate customs were respected and whose ruling chiefs preserved their own stools, or thrones, but who were subject to the suzerainty of the king of Ashanti—the Asantahene.

The Ashanti empire was never static or absolute, varying rather in its degree of central control and shading away from the pure Ashanti districts in the center to the less indoctrinated tribal areas on the perimeter. Nevertheless, the Asantahene became the most formidable indigenous ruler of West Africa, whose writ ran in one degree or another from the Black Volta to the sea.

The revelation of the Golden Stool consolidated this power by providing a supernatural focus of loyalty. Through its agency the Ashanti came nearer than any other West African people, except perhaps the people of Dahomey, to a concept of nationalism in the Western sense. Where the stool really came from, nobody knows. It was a wooden tripod partly sheathed in gold, and according to legend, it appeared from the skies during an assembly of the chiefs and people at Kumasi. Summoned by the great seer Anokye, it floated down from heaven in a cloud of dust, to the sound of thunder and the flash of lightning. It alighted on the knees of the Asantahene, and Anokye reverentially smeared it with a paste made from the nail clippings and hair cuttings of the assembled chiefs, announcing that henceforth the stool would be the embodiment of the Ashanti *sunsum.*

From that moment on, the stool took precedence over the Asantahene himself. It reclined on its side, as if in repose, upon its own chair of state, shaded by its own palanquin and attended by its own acolytes. It provided a constant factor in the continually shifting structure of the Ashanti state, and upon its mystique rests, even now, the fabric of Ashanti custom.

This was a civilization of some urbanity. Its polytheistic observances were intricate and devout. Its social forms, though based upon military need, were liberal. Its justice was based upon an elaborate system of oaths. The Ashanti were excellent craftsmen in gold, silver, and wood, and they developed their own architectural style, with projecting eaves, high-pitched thatched roofs, complicated plaster fretwork, and lively ornamentation of animals and birds.

Early Western visitors to Kumasi, in the first years of the nineteenth century, found the capital unexpectedly impressive. The Englishman T. Edward Bowdich, in 1817, reported a reception by bands of flutes, horns, and drums and by vast companies of warriors, resplendently accoutred with rams' horns, eagles' feathers, shells, leopards' tails, bells, amulets, blunderbusses, quivers of poisoned arrows, tasseled spears, and iron chains held between their teeth. The city he found well planned and scrupulously clean, with wide, named streets and carefully planted trees. Each house had its own lavatory, flushed with boiling water, and rubbish was burned daily. The royal palace, in the center of the capital, was a group of interconnecting courtyards covering some five acres. When Sir William Winniett was entertained at dinner there in 1848, he was given roast sheep, turkey, plum pudding, nuts, ale, and wine—"really," he commented with satisfaction, "very nicely served up."

But the root of Ashanti policy was a passion for power. "If power is for sale," ran an Ashanti proverb, "sell your mother to buy it—you can always get her back again." Ashanti na-

77

tionalism was aggressive and self-confident, and to the eyes of baffled Westerners, peering through the forests in the early decades of the Victorian era, the Ashanti kingdom seemed a dangerous and barbaric force. In particular, the Christian world shuddered at the Ashanti practice of human sacrifice. When an Asantahene died, scores, sometimes hundreds, of citizens were slaughtered to provide a ghostly retinue for the king. Most of the victims were criminals or prisoners of war whose lives had been saved for the occasion, but some were senior officials or royal relatives who had sworn to die with their ruler.

Every Ashanti generation knew this great communal rededication by death, and at times of war or crisis there were often *ad hoc* sacrifices of victims doomed on the spur of the moment. Like the Golden Stool, the practice gave cohesion to the nation, binding the past with the present, fate with

free will, the decrees of gods with the destinies of humans. In the developing world of Victorian enlightenment, though, no state bound by principles of such dread atavism could long hope to escape the tuition of those who, in their own groves and temples far away, had evolved very different versions of the only truth.

For more than a century after the descent of the Golden Stool Ashanti independence remained inviolate. There was probably nobody in central Ashanti who doubted the divine origins of the stool or the sacred privileges of the Asantahene; and though the convictions of the vassal tribes were less absolute, and there were often internecine squabbles and rebellions, still the confederation thrived. The arts and crafts of Ashanti flourished in the old way, and the life of the state remained enmeshed in the web of magic, tradition, *force majeure,* and military

skill that had raised it to power in the time since Osei Tutu and Anokye.

But in Africa the writing was on the wall—in European script, if only because so few of the African peoples had scripts of their own. Since the fifteenth century nine European countries, generally represented by chartered companies, had established trading stations along the West African coast, from Mauretania in the north to Nigeria in the south. The Portuguese, who built their first post in 1482, were followed by the Spaniards, the Swedes, the Danes, the English, the Dutch, the French, the Brandenburgers, and that forgotten people the Courlanders—Balts from southern Latvia. At first, none aspired to sovereignty. Their establishments were trading agencies, not government outposts, offering all manner of European manufactured products, from calico to firearms, in return for gold, ivory, and slaves. The Europeans paid court to the African

chieftains of the shore, and they had close professional connections with the entrepreneurs of the slave trade.

Nevertheless, they were emissaries of another civilization, and the forts they built upon the African strand must have seemed prodigious works to the tribespeople. Their prototype, the Portuguese fort at Elmina, was the model for trading forts, or factories, throughout the overseas empires of Europe, and it stands there formidably still. A surf-lined sandy beach stretches from it north and south, rimmed by palm trees, upright and aslant. At its foot lies the ocean; at its back the scrubby coastal plain runs away to the first wooded corrugations of the interior. A small town clusters subserviently near it, and gloriously massive above a bluff stands the great mass of its fortifications—curtain walls and buttresses, moats and drawbridges, ornamented gateways, colonnaded passages, turrets, gun platforms, bas-

tions, batteries, and chapels—like a colossal high-and-dry battleship, glowering on a foreign sandbank.

More than forty such forts and stations were built by the Europeans along the West African coast, and several of the most powerful were on the Gold Coast. This was the littoral of the Ashanti. The Ashanti did not directly control it, but they exerted a forceful and sometimes alarming influence over the Fanti tribes along the shore, and they periodically made claims to sovereignty—notably over Elmina itself. The presence of the Ashanti power, astride the trade routes from the interior, powerfully affected the trading process, sometimes forcing the coastal peoples into the arms of the Europeans, sometimes frightening them into opposition. It was clear that one day the Europeans would clash with this secretive and redoubtable kingdom of the forests: the Ashanti were hardly a people of compromise,

At the yam festival of the Ashanti in 1817, shown in a contemporary English engraving, vassal chiefs gathered under umbrellas to pay homage to their overlord, the king of the Ashanti, seated in the center under his stately red umbrella. Among his guests were British officers of the Royal African Company.

and the Europeans, as they approached the climax of their power, were in no mood to be thwarted by a pagan kingdom of repulsive habits.

The first serious collision occurred during the reign of the Asantahene Osei Bonsu—"the Whale"—who succeeded to the throne in 1800. By his time the principal power on the shore was Great Britain, represented first by the Royal African Company, later by a royal governor. From their headquarters at Cape Coast Castle the British had concluded a treaty with the Ashanti, but the relations between the two powers were bedeviled by side issues and misunderstandings. Lesser

RADIO TIMES HULTON PICTURE LIBRARY

tribes looked to the British for protection against Kumasi; refugees from Ashanti justice ran to the British forts. There were constant quarrels and skirmishes.

In 1822 war broke out, sparked by an exchange of insults between an Ashanti trader and a Fanti policeman. Each side attacked the other, the one blowing its war horns, the other playing "God Save The King," and the fighting continued on and off for nine years, leaving trade at a standstill and life along the coast chaotic. At one time the Ashanti army threatened Cape Coast itself, and in 1824 the British governor, Sir Charles MacCarthy, suffered an ignominious defeat and was probably beheaded. The Ashanti sent his skull triumphantly to Kumasi, where for years it was paraded on ceremonial occasions.

The Ashantis still remember this as MacCarthy's War, and recall the skull with nostalgia; but the British won the war in the end, and for sufficiently far-sighted seers it signaled the eventual fall of the Ashanti military machine and the humiliation of the Golden Stool.

For most of the rest of the nineteenth century the Ashanti were at war—directly with the coastal peoples over whom they claimed sovereignty, indirectly with the British, who had as-sumed the role of a protecting power. Relations between Cape Coast and Kumasi steadily deteriorated, neither side remotely understanding the other. The Ashanti thought the British thoroughly perfidious, the British considered the Ashanti as savages. With the abolition of the slave trade the British stood in a new relationship to the African peoples: strong evangelical lobbies argued for the suppression of such customs as human sacrifice, merchants and chambers of commerce demanded imperial action in the interests of profit. On the Gold Coast the British wavered, sometimes considering complete withdrawal, sometimes contemplating a wholesale conquest of Ashanti; while the Ashanti brooded over old grievances or marched here and there in inconclusive and inexplicable campaigns.

In 1872 the Dutch decided to withdraw from the Gold Coast, and sold their fort at Elmina, inherited from the Portuguese, to the British. This the Ashanti resented, because they claimed to own the fort themselves, and they accordingly crossed the River Pra, the traditional frontier of Ashanti proper, to besiege Elmina and Cape Coast. They were driven back, but the British now reached the conclusion that a grand imperial campaign was necessary, to settle the Ashanti once and for all and to achieve stability in the Gold Coast.

Of all the "little wars" of the Vic-torian era, this was the most classically perfect. It occurred at a time, shortly after the Franco-Prussian War, when the British Empire, by then the supreme exponent of the imperial idea, was flexing its muscles toward a climax. Morally, the British were in a mood of self-righteous assertion. Militarily, they were anxious to prove that they could match the superpowers of Europe. Politically, they were at the start of the imperialist crescendo that was to culminate in the frenzied New Imperialism at the end of the century.

The Ashanti, under the belligerent young Asantahene Kofi Karikari, were confident in their sacred cause, their traditional tactics, and their knowledge of the terrain. "The white man brings his cannon to the bush," they used to say, "but the bush is stronger than the cannon." On the other side, Victoria's armies were led by Sir Garnet Wolseley, who was to become W. S. Gilbert's "very model of a modern major-general"—ambitious, intellectual, socially correct, highly efficient, and, of course, deeply religious. He was only forty himself, and among the young officers who formed his staff were no fewer than nine who would later become generals. It was like a crusade against the black king, attended by the most shining of the queen's knights. "Remember," Wolseley told his soldiers, "that the black man holds you in su-

Curious British soldiers, opposite, gape at the place they called "Death Grove," where the Ashanti deposited their sacrificial victims. The Illustrated London News *printed this sketch in April, 1874, with a report on the expedition against the Ashanti. It was led by Sir Garnet Wolseley (right), who obtained a promise from the Ashanti to end the practice of human sacrifice. On his return to England, Wolseley was hailed as a conquering—and civilizing—hero, but the Ashanti weren't really beaten for another generation.*

perstitious awe; be cool; fire low; fire slow, and charge home."

An ultimatum was sent to the Asantahene—by traction engine, for effect. There was no official reply, though the leader of the Ashanti army, who had intercepted the British note, sent back a message that was, in effect, a counter-challenge. The British Army moved across the Pra into Ashanti, building 237 bridges as it went. It was a copybook campaign. As always, the Ashanti fought courageously, sometimes halting the action to make a propitiatory human sacrifice; but the shots of their muzzle-loaders often bounced off the enemy, and for all their jujus, spells of magicians, and incantations of priests, in six weeks they were beaten and a British army stood, for the first time in history, outside the Asantahene's palace in Kumasi.

Sir Garnet was a severe victor. He found Kumasi deserted, the Asantahene having taken to the bush, and he destroyed it. "Death Grove," where the troops cheerfully inspected the remains of the 120,000 victims supposedly sacrificed there, was burned. The palace was blown up. The royal treasure was auctioned off, and much of it was shipped to England by the officers who had bought it.

After two days Sir Garnet withdrew his forces, but messengers from the Asantahene overtook him, and at the village of Fomena the Ashanti submitted. They agreed to renounce all rights in the British zone, to pay a huge indemnity, to recognize the independence of four vassal peoples, and to do their best to end human sacrifice. The Ashanti remember this as the Sagrenti War, after the British commander. Sir Garnet himself went home in glory; he was awarded the Grand Cross of the Order of St. Michael and St. George and given twenty-five thousand pounds by a grateful Parliament—for had he not, as *The Illustrated London News* observed, successfully taken his troops into a "dark valley of the Shadow of Death" against a "warlike, crafty and ferocious nation"?

To the crafty and ferocious Ashanti the defeat seemed neither abject nor permanent. They were still independent, and the withdrawal of the British Army after only two days in Kumasi seemed to them to be a confession of cowardice. On the British side, too, once the trumpets had faded, the score seemed incomplete. The Ashanti empire had indeed temporarily fallen to pieces, but this led to more trouble rather than less—trouble between Kumasi and the provinces, between the coastal tribes and the Crown, between Briton and Ashanti.

So, in the last decades of the Victorian century, the Ashanti confrontation with the world drew toward its inevitable denouement. Events soon forced the British into action again. Other European nations had joined the grab for wealth and power called the Scramble for Africa; in particular, the French and Germans, with footholds on the West African coast, were seeking to turn the flank of the British Gold Coast by acquiring territories to the north. The conviction grew in London, despite opposition from radicals and anti-imperialists, that Ashanti must finally be annexed to the Crown. The Asantahene, declared the colonial secretary Joseph Chamberlain, was "a barbarous chief, who has broken the Treaty, permitted human sacrifice, attacked friendly chiefs, obstructed trade and failed to pay the fine inflicted upon him after the war: and the only proof he has ever given of civilization is to be found in the fact that he has engaged a London solicitor to advocate his interests."

A mission was sent to Kumasi offering the Asantahene, the eighteen-year-old Prempeh, the "protection of the Crown." Later, when he demurred, a British expedition once again crossed the Pra. Near Kumasi a messenger arrived to say that the Asantahene had changed his mind and would accept "white man's rule"; but it was too late, and the British Army sternly continued its advance toward the capital.

Sir Frederic Hodgson, left, touched off the last Ashanti uprising in 1899 when he demanded the surrender of the Golden Stool so that he, as governor of the Gold Coast, could sit upon it. To the Ashanti, this was the ultimate sacrilege, for they regard the stool not as a mere throne but as a living presence, and to this day they display it only on rare occasions of state. Its hiding place may be one of the old Ashanti fetish houses, like the one shown in the photograph opposite, which are magical abodes consecrated to the gods.

There then ensued the unhappiest of all the sad episodes that mark the enlightenment of the Ashanti. In the great square at Kumasi, on January 20, 1896, Prempeh, the queen mother, and the principal chiefs of the Ashanti nation were assembled in submission. All around were British troops with fixed bayonets. The governor of the Gold Coast, William Maxwell, accused the Asantahene of failing to answer his ultimatum and announced that he would be allowed to retain his throne only upon payment of an indemnity of fifty thousand ounces of gold—some two hundred thousand pounds—which was more or less the cost of the expedition and was far beyond the resources of the Ashanti. In any case, he added, a British resident would henceforth represent the imperial power in Kumasi.

Prempeh gave no reply. He slipped off his sandals, the traditional Ashanti gesture of deference, removed the golden circlet from his head, walked slowly across the square, and prostrated himself before the governor. "I now claim," he said simply, "the protection of the Queen of England." Surrender, though, was not to prove so simple. Prempeh offered to pay the indemnity in installments, but the governor replied that he must be given security for the balance. The Asantahene, he said, his mother, his father, his two uncles, his brother, his two war chiefs, and

three vassal chiefs would be taken as hostages "to the coast." They were immediately arrested, and when the army was withdrawn, blowing up a few temples on its way and leaving behind a resident in authority, the Asantahene was taken in a litter to Elmina, where he was temporarily imprisoned. Later, he was sent by sea thousands of miles away to the remote Seychelles, in the Indian Ocean, where he remained until 1924.

The Ashanti made one more attempt to assert their independence, as the great maw of imperialism swallowed their state. Deceived and humiliated, their king exiled and their religion emasculated, they clung more passionately than ever to the mythology of the Golden Stool, that reliquary of their self-respect, whose whereabouts they had, through all the miseries of war and defeat, steadfastly refused to divulge. The British understood at last the immense power of this object, and when, three years later, an Ashanti boy offered to guide them to its hiding place, the new governor, Sir Frederic Hodgson, himself accompanied an expedition to Ashanti to search for it. While his soldiers scoured the countryside, Hodgson and his wife, with a military escort, settled in the handsome red-brick fort that the British had built in Kumasi.

There he summoned another assembly. This time he told the chiefs that the Asantahene would never return to Kumasi, and he demanded the surrender of the Golden Stool: "Where is the Golden Stool? Why am I not sitting on the Golden Stool at this moment? . . . Why did you not take the opportunity of my coming to Kumasi to bring the Golden Stool and give it to me to sit upon?"

This speech makes the blood run cold. Hodgson, not by all accounts an especially insensitive man, clearly did not know what he was saying. He could not have realized that the stool was more respected than the Asantahene himself—that it was a venerated presence in its own right, not a mere symbol. It was upon the soul of the Ashanti nation that Sir Frederic demanded the right to deposit his buttocks. The Ashanti of Kumasi predictably rose in rebellion and besieged the governor and his lady in the fort. There they remained, in some discomfort, for two months, finally escaping in a sortie to the coast. The rebellion dragged on for a year, until the last of the insurgent leaders was packed off to join the Asantahene in his island exile.

It was the end. Ashanti was at last formally annexed by the British Empire and proclaimed a crown colony. So the power of the Golden Stool was broken, and this most fascinating of

West African kingdoms joined its peers of Zimbabwe and Zululand, Dahomey and Benin, in the limbo of the African past.

Neither the British colonial governments of the twentieth century nor their Ghanaian successors ever dared allow the nationalist power of the Ashanti to threaten the stability of the state. Attempts to reduce the office of Asantahene to the level of a local chieftaincy were defeated, however, by the undying loyalty of people throughout the old Ashanti confederacy. When Prempeh returned home after a quarter of a century, he was greeted by scenes of extraordinary emotion; his successor, Prempeh II, survived all the vicissitudes of national independence to die peacefully in his palace this past summer.

Military power and the practice of human sacrifice have disappeared, but in other ways the Ashanti life-style remains intact; as a community, a reservoir of pride and tradition, the Ashanti state survives to this day. By the end of their colonial rule the British had at last begun to understand what it was all about. In later years the Asantahene was treated with ceremonial respect—Prempeh II was made a Knight of the British Empire—and many of the looted treasures of Kumasi were returned from London. The king of

Ashanti remains the paramount chief throughout wide territories of the Ghanaian interior, and all the consequence of the Ashanti identity, its mingled mystery and flamboyance, is maintained to this day among the purlieus of Kumasi.

The Golden Stool reappeared in the 1920's, when its hiding place was accidentally disturbed by a gang of road builders, and some of its trappings were stolen; the British were accused of complicity, and the episode nearly caused another rebellion. Today it is hidden away once more, but on great royal occasions it is paraded with reverent ceremony through the streets of Kumasi: golden umbrellas swaying; great men slung with sacred totems and symbolic weaponry; the daughters of the royal household carried high upon the bare black shoulders of retainers; the Asantahene himself reclining in his immense golden palanquin; drums beating, horns blowing, the vast crowd pressing all about—sweep of cloth, flash of gold, an irrepressible wave of popular emotion. And above it, weirdly bulbous upon its receptacle, the ancient and ugly object, origin of so much passion, that Okomfo Anokye summoned from the skies long ago.

I do not know where it lies between processions, but I can imagine the place. There are within the Kumasi re-

gion a very few surviving examples of the old Ashanti fetish houses, which have survived imperial revenge and shifting taste and remain perhaps the most moving reminders of Ashanti constancy. They are strange little places—part shrine, part dwelling house, built in the typical Ashanti style around an open yard. A sacred tree may grow inside, and sometimes the mud walls are ornately decorated, with geometric patterns, with crocodiles, or leopards, or stylized human images.

The door of the shrine room is usually closed; outside it charms may hang, or there may be stools turned upon their sides to prevent their use by evil spirits. A hush seems to hang around the place, as though all its centuries of mystic meaning are embodied in the heat and the sun and the dust particles that loiter on the light. And in just such a reclusive closet, I dare say, somewhere in the forested recesses of the countryside, or on the shores of the baleful lake, the sage Anokye's Golden Stool is cherished now, instinct still with all the triumph and tragedy of the Ashanti.

There is little of the world that James Morris has missed, and we like to think that we have missed little of James Morris. His last article in HORIZON, *on Venice ("The Most Triumphant City"), appeared in the issue for Winter, 1970.*

ILLUSTRATIONS CONTINUED OVERLEAF

STICKS AND STOOLS

*Just as the spirit of the
Ashanti nation is embodied
in the Golden Stool,
so the spirit of each Ashanti is
embodied in his personal
stool, like the wood and brass
one shown at the right.
Every Ashanti child receives
a stool as soon as he is
old enough to crawl. At left is
an Ashanti "linguist-stick,"
a wooden rod covered
with gold leaf. Such sticks are
borne by "linguists,"
officials who serve as spokesmen
for Ashanti chiefs. The
carving shows one man helping
another climb a tree,
perhaps a token of the linguists'
supportive role.*

RECRUITS FOR THE DRUM CORPS

*Ashanti women carry roundheaded
wooden dolls, like the one below, to ensure
the birth of handsome sons;
dolls with rectangular heads are thought
to fetch pretty daughters.
At right is a wooden drum and its stand,
thirty-nine inches high, which
belonged to one of the traditional groups
of itinerant singers and dancers.
The drum stand, with its small family and
animals, is a work of art in itself.*

A key royal official was the executioner, left. With a malefactor's head crooked in his arm, he strikes an insouciant pose that calls to mind the Ashanti proverb: "Once a man has cut off a head he no longer fears anything."

WEIGHTS AND MEASURES

None of the four miniature brass figurines pictured here is more than three inches high; all were used by Ashanti goldsmiths as counterbalances in the weighing of gold dust and nuggets. The casting of these gold weights, which often depict homely scenes and proverbial sayings, was once a flourishing Ashanti folk art.

Both these gold weights depict medicine men, each standing cross-legged and clutching a chicken that he is about to kill. This act was part of a ceremony designed to cure disease and to combat crop failure and other misfortunes.

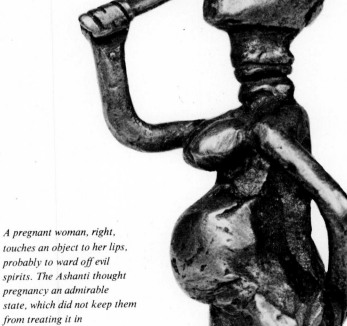

A pregnant woman, right, touches an object to her lips, probably to ward off evil spirits. The Ashanti thought pregnancy an admirable state, which did not keep them from treating it in an earthy, naturalistic style.

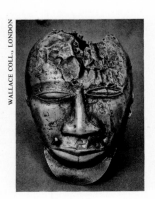

WALLACE COLL., LONDON

OVERLEAF: *The casting of a commemorative mask in pure gold marked the victory of an Ashanti over an enemy chief in war. The magnificent example, shown at left and on the next two pages, is only seven inches high, but weighs almost three and a half pounds. It is one of the few relics surviving from the once immense Ashanti treasure.*

Everything
You Always Wanted To Know
About The Dodo*

"Do not adapt too well to a comfortable environment, the dodo says. Do not become too fat. Do not lay your egg upon the ground"

There are people who put the dodo in a fabulous category, with unicorns, dragons, griffins, and centaurs—people like one of the guides at Syon House, the Duke of Northumberland's home near London, which I visited during a recent trip to England to look at dodo relics. Somewhere in Syon House a painting with a dodo in it was alleged to hang. "Oh, the dodo," the guide said, when I asked where the painting might be. "I don't know. I haven't seen it for two years. I think the dodo's gone."

When he inquired why I was interested in the painting and I began to explain, he was amazed that the dodo had actually existed, that it wasn't just a myth. The tolerant, amused smile that had humored my eccentric request faded a little. He called other guides and seemed to get quite worked up about it. In a little while the search was successful. The painting was found, hanging in a secretary's study, and after the guides had obtained permission from an august personage in a larger study, I was taken in to view the painting.

It was a very faint, flat thing, done in the early seventeenth century and attributed in the Duke's catalogue to one Melchior d'Hondecoeter and by other authorities to Jan Goeimare (the painting bears the initials J. G.). I saw a surrealist landscape of an island, the foreground crowded with large, Dali-like sea shells, the background a small bay with Perseus on a winged horse flying down to attack a twin-antennaed sea monster,

while Andromeda stands, an anxious captive, on the shore. The island is picturesquely and densely populated with birds: ostriches, ducks, geese, and, crouching on one side, a plump, dark-brown bird, fatter than a turkey, with a funny downcurved beak. You can see immediately why the guide might have thought the dodo fanciful. But you can also see why the painter, once having encountered a dodo, would have put it into his picture. The dodo lived.

The dodo lived on the island of Mauritius, in the Indian Ocean, four hundred miles or so east of Madagascar. The bare bones of the matter are that it lived there happily until Western man arrived, early in the sixteenth century. Presumably, before then, Arab traders in their dhows had called at the island, but hadn't disturbed the bird. The dodo, a sort of exaggerated dove, grew fat and comfortable. Its wings eventually became so small that it couldn't fly. It had a call like a tooth-billed pigeon, "kōō kōō," or maybe "dōō dōō," and laid one egg, the size of a breakfast roll. Having no enemies, it laid its egg upon the ground. The dodo was lean in the hot, rainy season, from October to March, and fat (weighing roughly fifty pounds) in the cool, dry months from March to October.

The Portuguese mariners on first arriving at Mauritius, tired of their ship food, called it *duodo,* simpleton, and the Dutch, arriving next, adapted this to their name for the little grebe, *dodaers,* fat arse. They also called it *Walghvögel,* nauseous bird. But after a diet of weevil biscuits the dodo was palatable. Captain West-Zanen and his large crew "made an ample meal of three or four of them with meat to spare." Matelief in 1606 said, "they are tolerable eating but the stomach is the best part." Sir Thomas Herbert in 1634 disagreed: "Greasie stomachs may seeke after them, but to

the delicate they are offensive and of no nourishment."

Whatever it tasted like, the dodo was vulnerable. A Dutch sailor wrote in 1631, "They are very serene and majestic, they showed themselves to us with an extremely dark face with open beak, very dapper and bold in their walk, and would hardly move out of our way." A crude engraving in West-Zanen's journal shows sailors clubbing dodoes to death. Pigs came ashore from the ships, as did rats. Dodo eggs lay, accessible, on the ground. The British East India Company official Peter Mundy saw no dodoes when he stopped at Mauritius in 1638 on his way home; by then they must have been scarce. The last direct mention is in the journal of Benjamin Harry, relating to the year 1681, when he says of the dodo that its "fflesh is very hard." In 1693 the Huguenot exile François Leguat made an inventory of the wildlife of Mauritius and neighboring islands, and made no mention of the dodo. He did, however, note the wild boars, which devoured "all the young animals they catch."

This downy, big-bodied, little-winged bird was the first species in recorded history clearly to become extinct through human agency. It was one of forty birds on the Mascarene Islands that are now extinct, but something about the dodo made it a special object of enthusiasm, devotion, and, perhaps, obligation. When, at the beginning of the nineteenth century, doubt was cast on the fact that it had ever actually existed, scholars rushed to their pens. Throughout the reign of Victoria scarcely a year passed without the publication of commentaries, learned notes, and now and then, a notable monograph. This industry was further fueled by the discovery in 1865 of a large number of dodo bones on Mauritius in a muddy delta called the Mare aux Songes

—1865, by the way, was the year in which *Alice in Wonderland* was published, and the dodo is one of the birds that fall into the pool of tears formed when Alice, nine feet tall, cries so much. (There is a nice, gentle association of author and character in the eleventh edition of the *Encyclopaedia Britannica,* where Charles Lutwidge Dodgson, who was Lewis Carroll, is the entry before Dodo.)

Before 1865 dodo devotees had to make do with even sparser evidence than those delta bones. By the time the species vanished, several dodoes had been shipped from Mauritius as curiosities: one perhaps went to Japan, two to India, one to Italy, at least half a dozen to Holland, and two, maybe, to England. One turned up at the court of the Holy Roman Emperor Rudolph II. And these birds left relics in various parts of Europe: a head in Copenhagen, a small upper mandible in Prague, tarsometatarsi in Leyden. In Clusius's *Exotica* there is an illustration of a dodo. The Dutch court painter Hoefnagel portrayed the bird. Roelandt Savery, the Dutchman who was also an excellent flower painter, made a subsidiary profession out of painting and drawing the dodo, and such other artists as Adriaen van der Venne (whose 1626 drawing seems to have inspired Tenniel's dodo in *Alice*), or the unknown craftsman who around 1561 embellished the gable of a house in the Dutch port of Veere with the figure of a bird resembling a dodo, found it a creature to conjure with.

Walking down a London street, probably around 1638, a gentleman called Sir Hamon Lestrange saw a canvas banner with the picture of a strange fowl on it. Taken by this advertisement, he went in and found a bird, which its keeper called a dodo, "somewhat bigger than the largest Turky cock." It swallowed nutmeg-sized pebbles to

*BUT WERE AFRAID TO ASK

assist its digestion. This was perhaps the dodo that was acquired, stuffed, by John Tradescant, who was not only a great horticulturist (he produced the first lilac, the first acacia, and the plane tree that graces our city streets) but a great collector. His museum of rarities, called Tradescant's Ark, was much visited by naturalists and the public at South Lambeth. In the Tradescant catalogue of 1656, in the section Whole Birds, is listed the "Dodar from the island Mauritius, it is not able to flie being so big."

John Tradescant, Jr., bequeathed this collection to a friend and lodger, Elias Ashmole, founder of the Ashmolean Museum at Oxford. There the dodo remained until 1755. In that year the university vice-chancellor and trustees of the museum considered what to do with the dodo, which was probably stuffed with salt and sand, by then altogether tatty, and, who knows, maybe lice-infested. In Ashmole's Statutes, No. 8, it said: "That as any particular grows old and perishing the Keeper may remove it into one of the closets or other repository, & some other to be substituted." The dodo was removed, and burned. Some thoughtful soul preserved the head and one foot, but there was, of course, no other bird to be substituted. The dodo was extinct.

Before I reached the Ashmolean on my recent pilgrimage, I called at the Zoological Society in London. The staff there was all helpfulness, soon finding me H. E. Strickland's classic monograph *The Dodo and its Kindred* (London, 1848) and the 1953 work by Masauji Hachisuka, *The Dodo and Kindred Birds,* which is dedicated to His Late Majesty Boris III of Bulgaria. For a few minutes I was permitted to have on my library desk the society's Savery, a lovely naive painting. It shows a dell by the edge of a marsh, with a few deer looking on as all sorts of birds plummet out of the sky. Savery wasn't very good at painting birds *flying.* Here eagles, parrots, storks, and ducks drop, stalling, to join their colleagues on the ground and in the water. The dodo sits in one corner, rather hunched up, as if he knew West-Zanen's hungry men were about to enter the picture.

I went next to Kensington to the natural history branch of the British Museum. After some initial hesitation on the part of the staff, I was taken to see a painting of the dodo, which hung in the bird curator's office. The curator was away, and the young man who guided me through obscure professional recesses of the museum said, "We don't get many people who ask to see it." I told him that the dodo entry in the latest *Britannica* was down to a few brief lines, after five columns in the eleventh edition. The painting, unsigned but once presumed to be by Savery, is a large profile view of the bird, not at all in Savery's somewhat miniaturist style. It might have been done by a Sunday painter who frequented Tradescant's Ark.

Upstairs again, I looked at the public display case in the bird wing, in which there is a fairly complete skeleton, put together from bones found in the delta deposits in 1865. There is also a life-sized imitation stuffed dodo, which seemed popular. Two young art students and one small boy were sketching it. Mothers were bringing their children to look at it. An old lady came and glared and said aloud, apparently to herself, "Obsolete creature!" It was a very friendly looking fellow, plump and burgherish, with a bony yellow forehead and bill, little black eyes, gray matted feathers, and a prominent fat rump, emphasized by several upstanding white tail feathers.

I had learned at the Zoological Society that these feathers had concerned the most recent serious inquirer before me, a "stuffer" from Rowland Ward, the famous taxidermists. So I went on to Mayfair to have a chat with Mr. Gerald Best, a director of the firm, who told me that Ward's had made a dozen dodoes in the last fifty years at a cost of two to three hundred pounds apiece. "No one else can do them," said Mr. Best. "It's a tremendous job, takes tremendous patience. A question of really sweating into the research, studying the books, paintings, skeletons. Then building up the body out of excelsior covered with plaster. Casting the beak and feet. Then the dyed pigeon feathers have to

be applied, one by one, using tweezers. They have to lie right. It sometimes takes a couple of years. It's very trying on the eyes and the men have to keep putting the job aside for a while and take it up again when they feel better."

In Cambridge they have the second best dodo skeleton in the world. They are also going to have one of the best modern museums of zoology. When I arrived, however, the old museum had been demolished and the new one was still dustily rising on the site. The exhibits were all over the place in borrowed quarters. A junior technician led me to the cupboard in the Metallurgy Department in which the dodo skeleton was stored: it had an S-shaped head-neck-spine assembly, tiny wing bones and huge drumsticks—a domestic fowl breeder's delight. The inner skull looked like dried-up honeycomb, and wire held together sections from which the ribs were missing. A stiff metal rod propped up the backbone and was fastened at the base to a round piece of oak, in need of varnish. There was a little label, *Didus ineptus,* the name given to the bird by the great eighteenth-century classifier Linnaeus. Clumsy Dodo. Nearby, several large boxes were packed full of what my guide called assorted spare parts, collected on Mauritius by Sir Edward Newton. (From such bones the best skeleton had been put together and shipped back to the dodo's homeland.)

A painting of the dodo that had hung in the corridor couldn't be found. But Professor Joysey, the curator of vertebrates, uncovered for my perusal Strickland's scrapbook. Like a modern filing cabinet, it contained notes, letters, and clippings concerning the semiprivate publication of his 1848 dodo monograph. There were letters requesting quotations from printers, a reply from Prince Albert's secretary saying that His Royal Highness would subscribe, and letters from the publisher in reply to querulous questions from the author about the correctness of the publisher's accounts. Strickland's book inspired a good deal of prose, poetry, and doggerel about the dodo. *The Athenaeum* reviewed the book

well, and the *Literary Gazette* said it was "invested with a halo of interest and science."

I had been told by a friend who had worked for the Ashmolean Museum that people there would not be very forthcoming about the dodo. They were still upset about having burned the last actual stuffed bird in 1755; a case of Homo sapiens becoming Homo ineptus. But here again, after an initial moment of incredulity and suspicion, the staff became enthusiastic. It was as though by helping me in my quest they were fulfilling an old obligation. Mr. James Hull, the Principal Technician of the Zoological Collection, found for me the dodo items, mounted on a piece of shabby black card, with the legend, The Head and Foot of the Last Living Dodo seen in Europe.

Below the skull was fixed the skin that had been removed from the left side of the head. It was rather like a piece of dried duck flesh, with a singed stubble of hair, and a black space, a hole, where the eye had been. I looked into that space. Extinction is a grandiose term, a hard-to-comprehend idea, but in this time of handy ethological comparisons between man and rats or man and apes, the dodo gives it meaning. Do not adapt too well to a comfortable environment, the dodo says. Do not become too fat. Do not lay your egg upon the ground. Do not lose the power of your wings. Mr. Hull, meanwhile, was saying that in 1755 it would have been difficult to preserve such a specimen once it started to decay. The Ashmolean had a problem in having lots of stuff that was uncatalogued or unidentified (for a while in the early nineteenth century it exhibited an elephant's leg bone as the thighbone of a giant), but nowadays it hung onto things because they might be valuable.

Mr. Hull felt a particular pride in whoever it was—perhaps a humble 1755 technician chap—who on being given the order to burn the old bird had saved these few bits and pieces.

The Tempesta Puzzle

Giorgione is counted among the world's great painters—but
only a handful of paintings are certainly his. The *Tempesta*
is his most famous work—but nobody knows what it means

Tempesta, 30¾″ x 28⅜″, GALLERIE DELL'ACCADEMIA, VENICE—SCALA

The enigmatic figures of the Tempesta *seem locked in private reveries, as oblivious to the breaking storm as they are to one another.*

Sometime in 1530 Marcantonio Michiel, an intelligent patrician who kept a sort of connoisseur's diary, jotted down the fact that in the house of the Venetian collector Gabriele Vendramin he had seen "the landscape with the tempest, with the gypsy and soldier, done by the hand of Zorzi da Castelfranco." Michiel thus became the first recorded viewer of the masterpiece that is usually, and perhaps incorrectly, referred to as the *Tempesta*. He also became, with his "gypsy and soldier" surmise, the earliest known practitioner of what might be called Tempestry, a form of divination that has been fascinating art experts ever since that time.

The fascination is understandable. The *Tempesta* invites and defies a decoding of its message. It is like a melody whose words you can never quite remember, a poem composed of unexplained metaphors, a still from an unknown motion picture. Moreover, the painting is part of a larger mystery: that of Giorgione himself.

Giorgio da Castelfranco—Zorzi, or Zorzo, in the breezy Venetian dialect—seems to have materialized on the Grand Canal in the early 1490's; he evidently came from Castelfranco Veneto, a small fortress town tucked into an idyllic landscape twenty miles north of Padua. He was a burly country boy with a tortured, histrionic face: in a self-portrait known through copies he looks like a long-haired Marlon Brando. According to Vasari's *Lives,* he was "very amorous." He may have spent some time in Giovanni Bellini's workshop, and in 1506 he shared a studio with Vincenzo Catena, a Bellini epigone. Documents dated 1507 and 1508 mention payments for a canvas in the Palace of the Doges and for frescoes on the façade of the Fondaco dei Tedeschi, the German merchants' hall near the Rialto Bridge. Late in 1510, when he was about thirty-two, he died of the plague, which Vasari says he

caught from "a certain lady" with whom he had been having "a very pleasurable affair."

A Giorgionesque cult swept through the Italian upper classes. A few days after his death Isabella d'Este, one of the most alert art patrons of her day, rushed a letter from Mantua to Venice in a vain effort to buy a "very beautiful and curious" Nativity that she had heard he had left unsold. The Venetian owners of two similar pictures refused to part with them "at any price." By 1524 the sophisticated Baldassare Castiglione in his *Book of the Courtier* was ranking the Castelfranco master with the *eccellentissimi* Leo-

This Giorgione self-portrait is perhaps a copy made during the seventeenth century. The artist died in 1510, in his early thirties.

nardo, Mantegna, Raphael, and Michelangelo. The diary of Michiel, written intermittently between 1521 and 1543, has sixteen detailed references to the new idol; and the list of admirers calls up sunlit visions of the best Venetian palaces and villas. By mid-century, with the addition of the *-one* suffix, Giorgio had become "Big George." By 1568 he could be cited in Vasari's second edition as having rivaled those "who were working in Tuscany and who were the creators of the modern manner," which was the highest praise a Florentine critic could imagine.

There would seem, then, to be little room for doubt that Giorgione was a remarkably poetic figure, somewhat in the tragic category of Keats, and also one of the great innovators in the history of Western art. He appears, from written evidence, to have provided a fresh impetus for the Venetian Renaissance and to have invented, for European culture generally, a new mode of feeling. But when we turn to the painted evidence, his personality and his achievement begin to blur alarmingly. There are no pictures bearing his signature. Worse, there are no works backed by contemporary documentation, for a fire destroyed the canvas in the Doges' Palace and marine air eventually reduced the frescoes to a batch of pink smudges.

Posthumous attributions are all we have. The majority of these are very posthumous indeed, and many are weakened by testimony that other hands, notably those of Titian, took over the dead innovator's unfinished projects. The sudden Giorgionesque vogue, which encouraged imitators, is another source of confusion; moreover, the possibility of unscrupulous "restorations" opens areas of suspicion that an earnest art lover can scarcely bear to contemplate.

If we ignore all these reasons for worrying, and count every hunch that has found its way into a catalogue, the number of acceptable attributions soars to above a hundred. If we are mildly insistent on scholarly agreement, the total drops abruptly to about a dozen. If we are finicky enough to demand an almost unanimous expert opinion, the only unquestioned works are *The Virgin with St. Francis and St. Liberale* (the latter may be Saint George), painted for a church in Castelfranco and still there; the *Tempesta,* now in the Venice Accademia; and *The Three Philosophers,* today in the Vienna Kunsthistorisches Museum. To these three, many experts would add the *Laura,* also in Vienna.

In the light of this disparity between the said and the seen, the *Tempesta* is

By ROY McMULLEN

more than a charming puzzle. It is, in many ways, the least conventional of all the paintings attributed to its creator and so possibly the most characteristic of his innovative "modern" style. With just a slight exaggeration, Kenneth Clark has called the picture "the one essential and indubitable Giorgione." If, then, we could decide what it is really about, we would have a better notion of what the whole Giorgionesque revolution, or revelation, was really about.

A gypsy and a soldier? The historians who have accepted this description tend, I think, to mistake archival priority for authority and to forget that Michiel, writing at least twenty years after the picture was painted, may have been guessing. Except for a certain wildness in her eyes, the woman does not look at all like a gypsy. Her nakedness and the white drape (it is not, as some adepts at gypsy Tempestry have alleged, a cape) suggest instead a figure of classical mythology or of Renaissance allegory. She is a sister of the similarly draped, and certainly nongypsy, nymphs in the Louvre's *Concert Champêtre,* which is usually assigned to Giorgione or to the Giorgionesque period of Titian. As for the man, well, he might be a soldier, though his rather unmilitary staff and his lack of armor and side arms make this unlikely.

Thirty-nine years after Michiel's visit an inventory of the Vendramin collection identified the man as a shepherd, presumably of the aristocratic variety found in pastoral romances. Modern scholars have objected that the staff is not a crook, that no sheep are in sight, and that Giorgione usually depicted shepherds as coarsely dressed rustics. The identification, however, does agree with cultural history. In 1504, a few years before the probable date of the *Tempesta,* the Italian revival of the classical pastoral convention had culminated in the publication of Jacopo

Sannazzaro's immensely influential *Arcadia,* familiar to students of English literature as a source for the poetic artifice, innocent sexuality, and idealized rural atmosphere of works by Sidney, Lodge, and other Elizabethans. Might it not also have been a source,

THE VIRGIN WITH ST. FRANCIS AND ST. LIBERALE

THE THREE PHILOSOPHERS

The two works above, together with the Tempesta, *are the only ones that almost all experts attribute to Giorgione. His style was frequently copied, and other artists, including Titian, completed some of his paintings.*

if only in a general way, for Giorgione?

In a nineteenth-century inventory, which may preserve a guess dating back to the Renaissance, the painting is listed as *Mercury and Isis.* Appar-

ently, the Egyptian fertility goddess was supposed to be nursing her son Horus during one of the trips that Mercury, actually the Greek Hermes, is said to have made to the region of the Nile. All this, in view of the setting and costumes, looks farfetched; and yet, in a mind a bit hooked on Tempestry, it can raise some nagging questions. Doesn't a nursing mother in a lush landscape strongly suggest fertility? Could those broken and obviously nonarchitectural columns, prominently situated in the near foreground, be the phallic symbols of Hermes? Could the vaguely aquatic bird that is roosting on a roof near the right end of the bridge be one of the cranes that in ancient times were sacred to the god? Could Michiel, during the learned talk in the palace of Gabriele Vendramin, have heard "gypsy," *cingana* in his spelling, when what was really said was "Egyptian," *Egiziana*?

Around 1880 the mythological approach was temporarily forgotten, and the whole splendid mystery went through a spell of Victorian sentimentalization and *embourgeoisement* from which the picture emerged as *The Family of Giorgione.* This numbingly domestic title can still be found in art encyclopedias on the shelves of otherwise respectable British and American libraries, in spite of the lack of a tittle of evidence that the painter was ever a husband, or even an unmarried father.

By World War I many experts began to look with favor on a suggestion made by the Italian historian Lionello Venturi: "The subject is nature: man, woman, and child are only elements—not the most important—of nature." This line of thought was later elaborated into readings of the work as an allegory of earth, air, fire, and water, as an illustration of the growth and decay principles in the universe, and simply as an allegory of the five senses, the thunderstorm being, presumably, very audible and the rich vegetation being fragrant.

Such general interpretations can seem altogether too general, and in the 1930's there was a return to specific anecdote and classical legend. Several scholars, among them the Giorgione specialist George M. Richter, felt that the painting referred to the myth of the infant Paris, who was exposed on Mount Ida because of a prophecy that he would be the ruin of Troy. This theory has the apparently fatal defect of leaving too many details, including the storm, unaccounted for, but it can stimulate a romantic imagination and interest Freudian speculators. Was Zorzi himself an abandoned or illegitimate child of an important father? Could this fact be one of the sources of his creative drive and one of the reasons for the veiled subject of the *Tempesta?*

The material for answering these questions is extremely fragile. No sixteenth-century document names the painter's parents; Vasari merely says that they were "humble." The painted evidence points only vaguely toward a "Paris complex," a preoccupation with forlorn infants. A "birth of Paris," which is listed by Michiel as one of the artist's earliest works, is known through a copy. A Giorgionesque picture that is now at Princeton shows a baby, probably Paris, abandoned in a landscape. A pair of Giorgionesque pictures in Milan depict the finding of Paris and his assignment to a nurse. Possibly related, in a psychological way, to the Mount Ida theme of the forsaken but divinely "chosen" child is the Uffizi *Ordeal of Moses,* a painting that experts usually attribute at least in part to Giorgione.

While the Paris theory was being debated, a vain attempt was made to identify the "soldier" as Adonis and the "gypsy" as Venus. A guess that the reference was to the career of Saint Geneviève as a shepherdess also failed to win approval. And then, in 1939, modern science added a fresh note to the discord: beneath the figure of the dreaming young man an X-ray examination revealed a seated woman with her legs in the water. Had she once had a role in the narrative? Was it possible that Giorgione had never had a narrative in mind and had just improvised an inhabited landscape? Or

LE CONCERT CHAMPÊTRE

The depiction of clad male and unclad female, which so shocked the nineteenth century when Manet exhibited his Déjeuner sur l'herbe, *can be traced to the* Tempesta, *and to this work, which some attribute to Giorgione, others to Titian.*

did the hidden bather prove only that he had thriftily made use of an old canvas?

In 1949 Kenneth Clark, meditating on the X ray and reflecting an opinion already widespread in Britain and America, decided that heavyweight Tempestry had demonstrated its futility. "The *Tempesta,*" he wrote in his *Landscape into Art,* "is one of those works of art before which the scholar had best remain silent. No one knows what it represents . . . and I think there is little doubt that it is a free fantasy, a sort of Kubla Khan, which grew as Giorgione painted it . . ." He

added that if we cannot say what it means, still less can we say "how it achieves its magical power over our minds."

This plea for passive enjoyment seems merely to have spurred erudite and clever spirits into venturing new guesses. During the next decade the painting was said to be about Moses, about Venus again, about the passion of Zeus for the nymph Io, who eventually became a heifer, and about the infancy of Dionysus—another forsaken divine child. The first two theories are open to the usual objection: they fail to account for enough of the picture. The third snags on the objection that, according to Ovid, Zeus approached poor Io not as a thunderbolt but under a thick cloud that hid his philandering from the jealous Hera. The fourth theory is not implausible. The thunderbolt could refer to the destruction of Semele, mother of Dionysus, by Zeus; the foreground could depict the sequel, in which Hermes turned little Dionysus over to the wet nurse Ino, Semele's sister.

Once again, however, the pictorial data scarcely warrants going beyond "could." Moreover, we now have a more impressive theory to consider. In 1969 Edgar Wind, whose studies of Renaissance pagan mysteries have ruined the hypotheses of many less knowledgeable art historians, entered the controversy with a short book lengthily entitled *Giorgione's Tempesta With Comments on Giorgione's Poetic Allegories.* In it he accepts the gypsy-and-soldier description, but maintains the picture is a "charade" rather than a "story."

He interprets the charade as a pastoral allegory in which *Fortezza* (fortitude, or constancy) and *Carità* (charity, or love) are placed in a setting of *Fortuna* (fortune, or chance). In support of this reading he points out that

the mother-and-child image was a common sixteenth-century symbol for *Carità,* that the word *"fortuna"* was a synonym for *"tempesta"* (it still is, in the sense of a storm at sea), and that broken columns like those behind the young man were familiar emblems of *Fortezza* in paintings done during the Renaissance—apparently because of an association with the fortitude of Samson in wrecking the pillars of the Philistine temple.

Is this pastoral allegory, after more than four centuries of scholarly hassle, the solution for the puzzle? Weary of irrelevant mythology, and possibly intimidated by Wind's masterful marshaling of iconographic parallels, we can be tempted to feel that it is. But I think we ought to look again at the picture, with eyes that are at once innocent and skeptical.

We find ourselves immersed in the peculiar silence, the strictly nonliterary atmosphere, that characterizes all great visual art. It is deepened by the stillness of a sultry Italian afternoon the moment before a thundershower breaks. Young alleged *Fortezza,* girlish in spite of his prominent codpiece, gazes languidly toward naked alleged *Carità* without seeming to see her; he may be just idly waiting for the sound that in a second, forever in the future, will rumble down from the distant lightning. Alleged *Carità* suckles her baby, if indeed it is hers, with an air of unsentimental habit and stares questioningly, rather brazenly, in our direction; she seems as unaware of alleged *Fortezza* as he is of her. Back of them stretches the town, a seedy but stately assemblage of Byzantine, Gothic, and Renaissance forms, many of which have no ascertainable function and all of which are apparently uninhabited. Everybody, the roosting bird included, is unconcerned about the coming storm, and understandably so, for alleged *Fortuna* is not much of a *tempesta.* An invading plant life, soon to be encouraged by rain, is on the march everywhere.

A 1939 X-ray photograph revealed that the male figure had been painted over that of a seated woman, a discovery that made the Tempesta *conundrum even more perplexing. Had Giorgione merely made thrifty use of a discarded canvas, or had this second nude played a major part in his original scheme?*

Would any unprompted viewer be likely to see the work as merely an allegory for a Renaissance cliché about constancy, love, and chance? As just a moralizing charade? No, Wind's explanation does not fit a real and total, as distinct from a rationalized, appreciation of the painting. It is inconsistent with what Clark calls "magical power." It is like saying that what Mozart's *Don Giovanni* is really about is the defense of maidenhood, or that the subject of Shakespeare's *Tempest* is political.

But isn't the explanation well buttressed with visible evidence, admirably reasoned, and in agreement with sixteenth-century practice? It is all of that, making important symbolic connections between the apparently incongruous man and woman, between them and the broken columns, and between the foreground group of motifs and the storm motif in the background. It supplies a structure that sticks in the mind much better than arrangements involving Isis, Adrastus, Zeus, and their like. So perhaps this explanation can serve as a point of departure for exploring what seems to me to be finally

the best "solution," which is nothing more than the common-sense proposition, advanced occasionally by exasperated experts, that the *Tempesta* has several levels of meaning. The fact that this solution is not really a solution need not bother us overmuch, for after all, a painting is not a puzzle. It's an experience.

The allegory of *Fortezza, Carità,* and *Fortuna* can be taken as the ground level of meaning, not only because it looks relatively solid and internally consistent, but also because Giorgione may have taken it as his own point of departure. Given the well-known customs of the time, it is not improbable that Gabriele Vendramin actually commissioned a painting built on the stock *Fortezza* theme, in line with a personal outlook or on the advice of a humanist friend.

However, I can see no reason to join Wind in assuming that the existence of an allegorical level of meaning automatically rules out the possibility of a narrative one. The Renaissance produced a multitude of pictures that can be regarded both as moralities and as stories, or at least as dramatic situations involving clearly identifiable figures and settings. Venus and Mars, for example, could simultaneously be Love and Strife; the fable of the Judgment of Paris could also be a Platonic sermon (and is discussed as such by Wind in another essay). Certainly a large number of sensitive people have thought that the *Tempesta* looked like a narrative picture, and their long quarrel over the nature of the story does not prove that the premise was a mistake. Something may yet turn up—most probably, in my opinion, something to do with Zeus and Hermes.

With the allegory of *Fortezza* and the unknown narrative stimulating his imagination, Giorgione very probably began to improvise. There is, of course, no proof that he did. But the alterations revealed by the X ray can be adduced, and so can some general evidence of his working habits. X rays of

Various interpreters have seen the young man opposite as a shepherd, a soldier, the god Hermes, and an allegorical representation of constancy.

The Three Philosophers show that several important features were changed in the course of execution. And Vasari, commenting on the frescoes for the Fondaco dei Tedeschi, complains: "But he thought only of demonstrating his technique as a painter by representing various figures according to his own fancy. Indeed, there are no scenes to be found there with any order . . . And I, for my part, have never been able to understand his figures nor, for all my asking, have I ever found anyone who does." The biographer, fortunately perhaps for his mental health, apparently did not see the *Tempesta* during his visit to Venice.

The improvising produced a level of meaning that can be called philosophical or lyrical, according to the viewer's temperament. On this third level the Venturi interpretation looks essentially right, as it does not on the allegorical and narrative levels: here, the subject is man integrated into nature—which is to say, that it is also nature integrated into man. The same subject appears in the Vienna portrait, which is currently entitled *Laura,* but which seems to refer less to Petrarch's mistress than to the Daphne who escaped Apollo's advances by being transformed into a laurel. The analogy with the *Tempesta* is rendered piquant by the circumstance that "Laura" is clearly the same woman, although a little heavier, who posed for the "gypsy." Was she the "certain lady," probably a Venetian courtesan, from whom the painter caught the plague?

On this third level a modern appreciator has to be wary of two traps. One is the mistaken assumption of a parallel with romantic mood landscapes,

Although the landscape of the Tempesta *is an imaginary one, the crenelated buildings, shown at right in a detail, are reminiscent of those in the artist's native town of Castelfranco Veneto. The mysterious beast that appears faintly outlined on the slablike building at the left has been interpreted as the dragon of Saint George, and hence as the emblematic "signature" of Giorgione.*

and the other, more treacherous, is the textbook commonplace that with the dawn of the Renaissance thinking people emerged from medieval spiritualism and confronted the reality of nature. A few did, but a scientific attitude did not really begin to prevail until the seventeenth century.

A Venetian intellectual of around 1507 (a fair guess at the date of the *Tempesta*) was likely to be interested in magic, alchemy, and astrology; in a revised Neo-Platonism mixed with Jewish theosophy and Egyptian or pseudo-Chaldean occultism; in Stoicism, which taught that God runs through the material world as honey runs through a honeycomb; and in the University of Padua's brand of Aristotelianism, which emphasized nature and held, among other heretical notions, that individual intellects were absorbed at death into the eternal intellect. Even a small section of this classical-oriental-medieval miscellany, sufficiently warmed in an artistic imagination, could yield a view of the universe that combined pagan pantheism with something close to primitive animism.

That the artist took such a magical view is another Giorgionesque proposition that cannot be proved. But *The Three Philosophers* shows that he was acquainted with the eclectic, esoteric doctrines of his time. In this profoundly meditative picture the bearded sage holds a sheet covered with celestial figures; the turbaned one is obviously an Eastern, possibly "Chaldean," seer; and the youth is manipulating a compass and a square as he raptly contemplates the countryside. Also, something like pagan pantheism could help to account for the weird heedlessness of the man and woman in the *Tempesta* —for their apparent readiness to be absorbed, mentally and almost physically, by natural elements. It could explain in part the lyrical storm, the encroachment of the pastoral landscape on the unreal, deserted town, and the work's whole air of being a sort of cosmic opera.

The operatic comparison puts us on

The model for this portrait of Laura, which many now believe Giorgione to have painted, seems also to have been the model for the nursing woman of the Tempesta. *Her low-cut gown suggests that she was a courtesan.*

the picture's fourth level of meaning, which seems to me to be best described as musical. Talk about this level must, of course, be entirely subjective and impressionistic, which makes many tough-minded scholars nervous; they are reminded of Walter Pater and the gemlike flames of the English aesthetic movement. But, in the first place, Pater's analysis of the Giorgionesque school in *The Renaissance,* including the famous observation that "all art constantly aspires towards the condition of music," holds up very well in a modern context; and in the second place, Giorgione actually was a musician.

We are told, again by Vasari, that he was "extremely fond of the lute, which he played so beautifully to accompany his own singing that his services were often used at music recitals and social gatherings." We can even be practically certain of at least one kind of music he sang and played, for his career coincided with the golden age of the *frottola,* which was the immediate ancestor of the Italian madrigal. The *frottola* was a relatively simple vocal form, suitable for performance by a group or by a soloist accompanying himself on the lute, and was often improvised. It was particularly popular among the literary gentlemen and grand ladies of the

Venetian region—among, that is, the same people who collected Giorgionesque pictures.

There is no need to go off the deep end with this sort of analogy. Much of Giorgione's painting technique can be explained quite adequately as a development of other painters' techniques. Nonetheless, there are subtle vibrations of brushwork, an unidentifiable aptness of transitions, and a tonality in the *Tempesta* that seem to be the work of an artist used to thinking and feeling in musical terms.

The same musicality can be found in representational aspects of his work, and here the comments of Pater, although not specifically on the *Tempesta,* are worth quoting at some length. Pater speaks of "exquisite pauses in time, in which, arrested thus, we seem to be spectators of all the fullness of existence, and which are like some consummate extract or quintessence of life." He evokes Giorgionesque music "heard across running water" and "people with intent faces, as if listening, like those described by Plato in an ingenious passage of the *Republic,* to detect the smallest interval of musical sound, the smallest undulation in the air, or feeling for music in thought on a stringless instrument, ear and finger refining themselves infinitely."

It can be objected that on this level the painting does not really have meaning, at least not in the same way that it has on the allegorical, narrative, and philosophical levels. But isn't the possibility of such an objection an indication of the thoroughly revolutionary nature of Giorgione's achievement in his own time? What he produced was a painting that was primarily a painting —a painting that had significance and emotional impact, but no more need of informational content than the music of a *frottola* had.

Roy McMullen, one of our most frequent contributors, is also the author of The World of Marc Chagall. *He is currently writing a biography of James McNeill Whistler.*

Giorgione's white-draped nude seems dreamlike and detached, even from her child, as if she belonged not to the real world but to myth or allegory.

"Chomsky is difficult to please."
"Chomsky is easy to please."
"Chomsky is certain to please."

Does language have a universal grammar? Yes, says this eminent practitioner of
the science of linguistics, and it may give us a clue to the essential nature of man

As a boy of nine, in 1938, Noam Chomsky used to sit in the front row of the Hebrew class at Mikveh Israel, in Philadelphia, paying little attention to the teacher.

He was not disrespectful, but he had covered the ground long before, at home, with his parents. His mother was the teacher in this class, and his father was the school's principal. I was a backward classmate, aged thirteen.

As a young boy, Chomsky used to proofread his father's work on medieval Hebrew grammar. It was only natural—one might say almost genetically fated—that he became interested in linguistics. Since he was no less interested in man's place in the world, he almost quit the University of Pennsylvania as a sophomore to go to Palestine and live on a kibbutz (he knew Hebrew and was studying Arabic).

If he happens to be the most famous professor of linguistics in the world, that is in part because his work in the field has been original, even revolutionary. It is also because of his second passion—an overpowering interest in politics and recent history. He is a ranking theorist and polemicist of the

At the blackboard of his M.I.T. office,
Noam Chomsky maps out his linguistic rules.

New Left, a determined opponent of the Vietnam war. This less scholarly eminence followed closely upon publication of an article, in *The New York Review of Books* in 1967, that dealt with the political responsibility of American intellectuals. In 1969 his political essays were published in *American Power and the New Mandarins.* He is constantly importuned for articles, statements, speeches—and his work is an extraordinary amalgam of the polemical (Chomsky on Songmy) and the esoteric (Chomsky on the Algebraic Theory of Context-Free Languages).

At the Massachusetts Institute of Technology, where he is the Ferrari P. Ward Professor of Modern Languages and Linguistics, Noam Chomsky could pass as an aging student. His office is unkempt and weary—torn green shades, dusty volumes, a chair in the final stages of disintegration—but he presides with blithe unconcern over such externals, and with intense devotion to what he considers essentials.

One must listen carefully when he speaks, not only because of the complexity of his thought, but because—having mentally reviewed his own reasoning so often—he tends in conversation to omit some intermediate steps.

What is more, he speaks very softly.

"Linguistics," he says, "is concerned with the description of a particular language, so its fundamental concept is the knowledge of a language. And a person who knows a language has somehow mastered a system of principles that determine the sound and meaning of infinitely many sentences."

"New sentences often pass between us—but we understand, and this is perfectly normal. What's exotic is repetition of old sentences." There are few examples of simple repetition in ordinary speech. Though there are stereotyped expressions, such as greetings, these are incidentals and do not overwhelm the characteristic inventiveness of speech.

"It's often said that language and other aspects of human behavior involve habit structures. But you can't innovate by habit. The first task of a linguist is therefore to grasp and characterize what makes innovation—that is, normal usage—possible; what allows us—free of detectable stimuli, external or internal—to speak our minds in an original, appropriate, and coherent way."

The linguist tries to make explicit what the child grasps intuitively, and therefore tries to construct a "generative grammar"—a system of rules and principles that determine the connection of sound and meaning for the indefinitely large number of sentences that constitute a single language.

But the linguist also tries to establish the principles of "universal grammar," which governs all human languages. As Chomsky explains: "Universal grammar tries to specify the constraints and principles which determine what makes a possible system of grammar into a humanly accessible system. It tries to distinguish the essence of human language from arbitrary systems that might be imagined."

But what leads Chomsky to believe there is an essence? He replies: "The best evidence is the very fact that a child acquires knowledge of a language—an astonishing feat which is beyond the capacity of an otherwise intelligent ape." Chomsky holds that language has not evolved from simpler systems in nonhuman organisms. The child acquires and constructs for himself a very specific generative grammar and does so, on the basis of degenerate and limited data, in an extremely short time.

"The data are degenerate in the sense that a good deal of the material that the child hears is not even properly constructed: normal language consists very largely of false starts and fragments and hesitations. But the grammar the child constructs tells him what is a well-formed sentence and how such sentences can be used and understood.

"The child is in a much worse situation than a scientist who experiments and has good data—he is rather like a physicist who can do no experiments but nonetheless tries to construct theories about the world. The child develops a very complex and articulated theory of enormous predictive scope and explanatory power—he takes an incredible inductive leap."

Chomsky suggests that the child brings to this enormously difficult problem "a very rich system of expectations—a very rich innate system that tells him how to interpret data as a possible language." He argues that if a child were initially uninformed as to the nature of the system he has to construct, if his mind were totally plastic—as the behavioral psychologists believe—the acquisition of language would be a miracle. Since he rigorously refuses to believe in miracles, Chomsky has another explanation. He says that the mind of a child is not plastic, but has intrinsic properties that are the subject of universal grammar.

Chomsky's work in linguistics is a highly complex attempt to fill in the details for the particular grammar of English and for a universal grammar for all possible languages. His work with the grammar of English is much less controversial than are his theories about universal grammar and its significance for a theory of mind and psychology.

What he has attempted to show—in opposition to earlier "structural linguistics" and behavioral psychology and indeed the whole tradition of empiricism in psychology—is that the principles of a grammar are deep and abstract, and that only an organism initially (i.e., at birth) informed of the nature of these principles (in fact, "preset") could have discovered them in a particular case. Such principles tell us something about the intrinsic nature of the human mind and define one capacity of that mind: the language capacity.

All of this puts Chomsky at odds with an older linguistic tradition that holds there is nothing universal about the form of language, and that the collection of sounds that transmit meaning is arbitrary rather than mind-determined, the result of environment and teaching rather than of natural structure. Though the earlier tradition has accumulated lots of material from particular languages, Chomsky maintains that it fails to ask or answer the really hard questions.

Had such iconoclasm been discussed within the confines of a linguistic dis-cipline, it would have created much less fuss. Chomsky's views have aroused academicians because of his repeated intimations of generality—the suggestion that his approach is the right one for other aspects of human behavior, such as ethics, psychology, aesthetics, sociology, and logic.

Thus he says: "Universal grammar is a hypothesis about the essential nature of man—what it means to be a human being, what psychology is about. It tells you it's hopeless, or at best marginal, to try to explain anything about humans in terms of habit formation, or stimulus and response, or associations, or the shaping of behavior by environment. It tells us that we don't acquire knowledge the way empiricists think we do—through experience by association of stimuli, stimulus-response connections, and training. Language is not a matter of know-how established by habit.

"If you want to find out what it means to be a human being, you have to examine free creation within a system of rules, acquisition of knowledge within the framework of restrictive conditions imposed by the mind. The human mind is thus a kind of schematism, or framework, within which learning and behavior take place. Linguistic competence—knowledge of a language—is an abstract system, a generative grammar, consisting of rules or constraints that determine the form and meaning of an infinite number of sentences."

To show what he means by constraints—or innate principles—Chomsky proposes two simple sentences:

(1) Mary believed (that John had read *the book*).

(2) Mary believed (the claim that John had read *the book*).

The general rule for forming questions is to take the italicized phrase, replace *the book* by *what book,* put it in front of the whole sentence (while making some adjustments of the main verb, i.e., replacing "believed" with "did . . . believe"). This works for (1) and gives us: what book did Mary believe that John had read? But it does not work for (2), since it gives us: what book did Mary believe the claim that John had read?

"I wouldn't say," explains Chomsky, "that the 'corresponding question' in the second case is 'What book did Mary claim that John had read?' Rather, that is the question corresponding, by the rule just mentioned, to 'Mary claimed that John had read the book.' "

"In fact, there is no question corresponding to (2). The problem is, how do we know this: how do we know that the simple rule just stated, which works for (1), doesn't generalize to (2)?

"The answer is that the italicized phrase, which is a noun phrase, appears within the parenthesized noun phrase in (2), but not within a larger noun phrase in (1)—rather, there the parenthesized phrase is a sentence. But the parenthesized element in (2) is just an extension of the noun phrase 'the claim.'

"There is a general principle that a noun phrase cannot be extracted from another, larger noun phrase containing it. Therefore the italicized phrase cannot be extracted from the parenthesized phrase in (2), but it can be in (1)."

Having said all this, Chomsky concludes: "The example demonstrates two important facts. First, in producing and understanding sentences we make use of abstract mental representations, such as the one indicated by the parenthesization in (1) and (2)—with the further information that the parentheses in (1) bound a sentencelike element and in (2) a noun phrase. Second, we operate with general principles; for example, you can't extract a noun phrase from within a larger noun phrase."

Retracing his argument, Chomsky is intent on showing that there is no question corresponding to (2). Thus, the sentence "What book did Mary believe the claim that John had read?" is one that we don't accept; indeed, it does not even occur to our mind to say it. In Chomsky's view this is evidence that there are general principles that

guide us—though we may be unaware of their guidance.

(Indeed, when Chomsky said the sentence aloud, I *heard* it as "What book did Mary believe that John had read?" He found this further corroboration for his argument, pointing out that my mind had kept me from repeating the sentence as it was uttered. My sixteen-year-old son, who was with us, told me afterward that Chomsky himself had said the sentence as I reproduced it; I therefore suspected that Chomsky's mind had not allowed *him* to say it as he wished. Since there was no neutral observer present, we will all have to remain in the dark. But the mistake *was* made, and it is characteristic of the principle.)

The language learner has no *evidence* for any such general principle. It is unimaginable that every speaker of English has been explicitly taught that he can't form a question from (2), or explicitly taught the general principle that determines this fact, or explicitly given sufficient information to demonstrate this general principle. Rather, he just hears such sentences as (1) and (2) and lots of others and develops a knowledge of language that is governed by these general principles, which are an innate part of the structure we impose on experience.

The acquisition of knowledge is therefore a creative act by which we impose on data a structure of principles. That structure determines what we come to know on the basis of those principles. We come to know that one collection of consecutive words is a sentence and another is not.

The principles are a skeleton, and the degenerate data of language is flesh concealing the skeleton. English and all other languages have the same skeleton, Chomsky and his followers argue, and the different varieties of flesh hang where the skeleton allows them to hang, not at random.

In universal grammar the skeletal principles are unconscious, and often there seems no way to pry them into

consciousness. Chomsky maintains, indeed, that the greatest defect of classical philosophy is its assumption that the mind's properties and content are accessible to introspection. This may sound obscurantist; Chomsky argues that it is realistic.

He returns to the blackboard. "When you hear a sentence you hear a noise," Chomsky notes, picking up a piece of chalk, "and when you look at the sentence you see words. But you know more."

To clarify this point, he writes down three additional collections of words that we call sentences:

"John is difficult to please."
"John is easy to please."
"John is certain to please."

In the first two sentences John is the person being pleased; in the third, John does the pleasing. The surface structure thus does not always reflect the deep structure—which relates not to the sound but to the meaning. Our knowledge of the difference is unconscious and a part of the structure of the mind, Chomsky says.

"One is not merely interested in the data of English, but in what it tells us about the structure of the mind. The mind is arranged in terms of principles of this kind—basic rules which determine systems of grammatical relations and the way to organize these deep structures into surface structures. How to determine the nature of these grammatical relations is a problem of science—difficult but not impossible."

Chomsky writes another sentence on the blackboard:

"The man will win."

The corresponding question is: "Will the man win?"

Then he writes: "The man who will arrive at six will win."

The corresponding question is: "Will the man who will arrive at six win?"

"How do I know that I take the second 'will' to form the question?" asks Chomsky, turning to his audience of two. "How do I know the question should not be formed by taking out the first 'will' and using it as the first word of the question: 'Will the man who arrive at six will win?' "

To answer his own questions, he proposes two possible formulations of the rule: first, take the left-most occurrence of "will," and put it at the head of the sentence; and second, take the occurrence of "will" that functions as "main verb" following the initial noun phrase of the sentence and invert it.

"Both rules give the same result in the case of the simpler sentences," he notes. "They give different results in the case of the longer sentence. The first, of course, gives the wrong result. But the first is by far the simpler rule. Suppose, say, you had a computer that was to perform these operations. To perform operation one, the computer would simply have to scan the sentence from left to right until it came across an occurrence of 'will,' which it would then prepose. To perform operation two, the computer would have to analyze the syntactic structure of the sentence, determining that 'the man who will arrive at six' is the noun phrase subject and 'will' is the main verbal element."

"Operation one is 'structure-independent'—it cares only about the actual content of the sentence to which it applies and doesn't care at all about its abstract structure. Operation two is 'structure-dependent'—it cares about the abstract structure of the sentence, as well as about its actual content. Though structure-dependent operations are more complex and abstract, languages appear to have only operations of this sort."

Nobody who has spoken English has ever made the mistake of opting for the first rule instead of the second, he says. "And why not? Why does our mind use a difficult rule instead of a simple one, and why does the rule apply in every language?"

His answer is that the structure of the mind tells us which operations are permissible and which are not.

In any language there are things we learn. In English, for example, we learn

that a rational featherless biped is "man," and in French we learn to call this animal *"homme."* But there are things we know without learning—such as the rule illustrated in the questions about the man who will (or will not) arrive at six.

The underlying pattern of the mind even provides us with a guide to pronunciation. If we kept only to the phonetic surface form, we could not understand why, for example, we should expect a full vowel in "rel*a*xation," and a reduced vowel in "dem*o*nstration," in the italicized position. In other related forms both these vowels are full rather than reduced: compare "rel*á*x," and "dem*ó*nstrative." In fact, as the examples "rel*á*x" and "dem*ó*nstrative" indicate, the vowels are full when they receive the main stress in the word. But in "rel*a*x*á*tion" and "dem*o*nstr*á*tion," the italicized vowel is unstressed in both cases, yet it is full in the first case and reduced in the second.

The reason is that "rel*a*x*á*tion" is derived from the underlying form "rel*á*x" and "dem*o*nstr*á*tion" is derived from the underlying form "d*é*m*o*nstrate," and in these underlying forms the italicized vowel of "rel*á*x" is stressed, hence full, while the italicized vowel of "d*é*m*o*nstrate" is unstressed, hence weak. In "rel*a*x*á*tion" and "dem*o*nstr*á*tion" the italicized vowel is unstressed in both cases, but in speaking and hearing these words, we make use of the abstract mental representation of the underlying form, with its stress pattern and consequent choice of full or reduced vowel, and in this way we determine the stress and vowel quality of the words "relaxation" and "demonstration" themselves. It turns out, then, that we hear and speak many words as if we had in mind their underlying forms.

There are probably similar things to be said about meaning, Chomsky suggests, adding, however: "We have ways for describing sounds, but we still don't have good ways for describing meaning."

"Everybody thinks his own field is the most important," Chomsky says smilingly. "Linguistics, however, does tell us interesting things about the nature of human nature, about the human mind and some of the conditions of human creativity and free thought and expression. It tells us how humans speak and understand and think, though it has not yet managed to relate its discoveries to physiological mechanisms or interpret thought in terms of 'physical causes.' "

"One might consider linguistics as a branch of psychology," Chomsky adds. "Take psychology generally. As a human being you have friends and acquaintances and have made some assessment about them, you have a theory about them, even if unconscious, about how they will act. An important part of psychology ought to be to state the theories and discover how you arrived at them. To do so, psychology should try to discover those intrinsic properties of the mind that lead us to interpret the insignificant data of experience to form rich conclusions about what people are like. I think we'd then perhaps discover something like a universal grammar not of language but of human nature."

"Psychology should thus ask: what is it we learn? Then it should ask: what is the universal system of constraints that made possible this learning? Psychology has suffered from the fact that it lacked the concept of 'what is known,' 'what is learned.' Behaviorists talk only about relations between stimulus and response. They offer no way to account for the fact that we speak intelligibly. Because of that conceptual gap, they haven't made progress."

Chomsky indeed finds it significant that we speak nowadays of "behavioral science," not of "science of the mind." It is as though, he suggests, we called natural science "the science of meter readings."

"Consider the acquisition of scientific knowledge," he says. "I'd assume there are some rather general conditions. I think that science arises when the structure of the world and the structure of the mind somehow fit together. Where the real nature of the world is such that it doesn't mesh with the structure of our mind, we don't have science."

"In science we sense intuitively that sometimes we have scientific knowledge and sometimes only intellectual technology. The difference can't be explained in terms of prediction. It has to do with comprehension, and psychology might attempt to specify the difference between scientific understanding and technology. The explanation would have to grow out of the concept of mind, and would be related to the kinds of intellectual structures our mind can produce."

Characteristically, Chomsky had to interrupt our conversation to attend a meeting of dissident professors at M.I.T. His colleague Morris Halle—who collaborated with Chomsky on the enormously difficult and technical book *The Sound Pattern of English*—replaced him on the dilapidated chair.

"What Chomsky has done is invent a kind of formal structure in terms of which you record your observations," said Professor Halle. "When Mendeleev invented the Periodic Table he told people to arrange chemical elements in a particular way. People said: 'Why shouldn't we do it alphabetically?' Mendeleev said the reason you should do it this way is because you will discover other things by doing this."

"One of the striking things was that they found holes in the table and errors in weights of certain elements—errors found in terms of his structure. They could then correct the errors, discover the reasons for them, and hunt for missing elements.

"This is what has happened in linguistics. There's a formal structure in terms of which facts are organized, and this structure allows you to organize additional facts.

"*Finding* facts is no problem. You can easily discover that the word 'America' is stressed on the second

syllable. But that fact is interesting only if it tells you something about structure. What you're trying to understand in chemistry is the nature of matter, and what you're trying to understand in linguistics is the nature of language.

"Just as you can find out lots of facts about chemical elements, the interesting question is how they're related, what do they mean, and this comes only when you invent a theory. It tells you about things you have never seen.

"In chemistry you discover the elements you didn't know. In language the things you discover are things you know—unconsciously. If what we're describing is a realistic description of language, the man on the street must 'know' how to use the machinery even if he is not conscious of its existence.

"He uses linguistic transformations without ever learning that such things exist. He doesn't learn that there are other things called phonemes, though he uses them all the time in speech. How does he manage to speak so fluently while he understands so poorly? Chomsky's answer is that this ability depends on an innate structure."

Halle, like Chomsky, reaches across to psychology to make the meaning clearer. A cat presumably sees a chair, yet a cat doesn't learn intellectually. How does the cat discover that there are objects such as chairs or people or other cats? The only reasonable explanation, says Halle (following Chomsky), is that this knowledge of objects is built in.

Analogously, pursues Halle, part of the genetic equipment of man is the ability to perform the activity called language use. "We've studied hundreds of languages," Halle notes. "We find differences in them, of course. But the deep properties, like transformations and phonemes, are in all languages."

"Until Chomsky came along, the dominant school in linguistics was structural. The idea was that you could find out relevant facts in language by comparing almost identical cases. To

show the difference between *t* and *p*, for example, you might offer 'tick' and 'pick.' The idea was that differences in sound that don't signal differences of meaning don't count, and you can ignore them. But our idea is that the important thing is for linguistics not simply to accumulate facts, which you can cherish as an antiquarian would, but to develop theoretical explanations for evidence. Grammar used to be 'natural history' and we are trying to make it 'natural science.'

"Just as chemistry tells you what structure a possible element must have, an element that we have seen as well as one yet to be discovered, linguistic theory defines a possible language, indeed every possible language. It thus tells you about thought, about behavior, about what it means to be a human being making choices through the filter of the mind."

Professor Halle waved one hand as though he wanted to seize the essence of thought within his fist and present it to me. "The use of language is certainly the most complicated intellectual process accessible to every man of normal intelligence," he said, "so it stands to reason that it may lead to an understanding of other intellectual processes, for example the ability to reason and to make computations."

"The most obvious field in which we can expect advances is psychology, and some people are already trying to apply the methods of linguistics in studying myths. Unfortunately, every field demands a different approach, not slavish transfer of a method that happens to work elsewhere. The example of the invention of particular methods to solve linguistic problems should spur scientists in other fields to devise methods applicable to their own problems."

Chomsky has no way of knowing how successful these efforts will be, and indeed, he has no desire to be a prophet. These days it is difficult enough merely to be a revolutionary.

Israel Shenker, Chomsky's classmate, is a writer for The New York Times.

The Scoundrel Who Invented Credit

John Law in his heyday. The scroll reads, in Latin, "I report my labors to the king."

A Scottish libertine
named John Law rescued France
from ruin, and ruined
her again, by basing prosperity on
credit. He showed us
the future, and it didn't work

By MORRIS BISHOP

John Law was born in Edinburgh in April, 1671. His father was a goldsmith and a moneylender as well, for goldsmiths often found it more advantageous to lend their gold than to work it. The boy was a brilliant student, especially in mathematics, and a tennis champion. His father having died, he set off at twenty, with an important sum in pocket, to try his fortune in London. He was tall, handsome, red-haired, with a large aquiline nose, a compelling bass voice, and gracious manners. "Beau Law," he was called. He used his powers of persuasion to bewitch lovely ladies, and also cards and dice.

Adventurers must accept their portion of misadventure. Law enjoyed the favors of a Mrs. Lawrence, at the expense of a Mr. Edward Wilson. According to the most savory of the story's several versions, Wilson was old, painted, bald but bewigged, and rich, gadding about in a six-horse coach. The lady wrote Beau Law jocular notes belittling Mr. Wilson's amorous efforts. Indiscretion led to divulgation, divulgation to a duel in Bloomsbury Square, and the duel to the death of Mr. Wilson. Law was jailed, tried, and condemned to death, but through the machinations of a great lady he was spirited out of prison and out of England.

In Amsterdam Law became secretary to the English resident. He observed with fascination the operations of the Bank of Amsterdam and the process of making money out of money. With pockets well filled, he returned to Scotland in 1700. Shocked by the poverty of his native land, he proposed to establish a national bank, which would collect public revenues and control manufactures, fisheries, etc. But the cautious Scots balked at his grandiose ideas. He left for the Continent, accompanied by Lady Catherine Senor, sister of Lord Banbury. The pair visited the courts of Europe, supporting themselves by their skill at faro, basset, omber, and loo.

In 1705 he published a remarkable booklet, *Money and Trade considered, with a Proposal for Supplying the Nation with Money.* Gold and silver, he said, were losing value by their abundance. He proposed that Scotland issue notes based on land. Credit, he went on, is a kind of money and should be so managed as to produce prosperity. Banks could impart a real value to paper, which would replace gold and silver for common exchange.

In 1707 the couple came to Paris, then under the shadow of grim old Louis XIV. Law kept the faro bank in the house of the wanton elderly actress, la Duclos. His style was much admired. With two sacks of gold at his feet, he won or lost with an imperturbable smile. He encountered in a bawdyhouse—so gossip says—Philippe d'Orléans, nephew and son-in-law of the king, and there, amid chatter and pouts, expounded his financial theories. These he developed in lengthy reports, asserting that wealth could be better created by governmental action than by the free play of individual enterprise.

But Law's own excess of individual enterprise annoyed the police; he and Lady Catherine were expelled from France as undesirables. They went to Italy, making their headquarters in Venice, the amphibious Las Vegas of eighteenth-century Europe. Law won steadily at games of hazard, and is said to have used private information from Paris to speculate in international exchange.

In August, 1715, at the news that Louis XIV was pushing at death's door, Law returned to Paris with his head full of projects and his coach groaning with gold worth a million and a half francs. The king died on September 1, and was buried amid scenes of shameless popular rejoicing. He was succeeded by his five-year-old great-grandson, Louis XV. Philippe d'Orléans, John Law's old companion, was named regent of the kingdom. He found finances in a calamitous position. The old king, who *was* the state, left a total indebtedness of three billion francs. The treasury was empty; the anticipated revenues for the two coming years were already discounted and spent. The regent and his advisers seriously considered declaring the realm bankrupt.

John Law now came galloping to the rescue of France. He proposed to create, with his own funds, a private bank, guaranteeing to pay off the government debt in twenty-five years. But he must have a free hand to put his revolutionary ideas into practice.

The few banks already existent in Europe were either banks of deposit, safeguarding money, or discount banks, accepting merchants' promises to pay and issuing against them their own promises, or notes, and limited to specific transactions. Law proposed a bank that would engage in business, collect state revenues, hold monopolies, and offer profitable investments. It would issue bank notes, paper promises, which would circulate everywhere in place of gold and silver. The bank notes would be secured by a gold reserve and by the country's credit, or its ability to furnish labor and goods. Prosperity would ensue, for, Law insisted, money creates trade: "we need more money to employ more people." If money is a representation of wealth, money is also a force, which may be manipulated to make wealth. The essential is credit, or faith. But credit, say some economists, is merely suspicion asleep.

The dazzled regent and his council believed Law's promises and accepted his proposal. The Banque Générale opened in June, 1716, with a capital of six million francs. Shares of the capital were eagerly bought. The bank issued its new bank notes, legal tender for all payments, convertible into specie at the holder's will, and handsomely engraved. Paris was delighted with the novelty and convenience of the notes, the relative security of a paper hoard against thieves. The notes were soon quoted at a premium over specie. And the abundance of money did indeed stimulate a revival of commerce.

Law now revealed the second part of his great project, which he always referred to simply as "the System." More generally it was called "the Mississippi." To provide a commercial base for his bank, to pay its dividends, he created a great holding company, the *Compagnie des Indes,* which obtained the monopoly of French seagoing trade and of the tobacco business, the operation of the royal mint, and the ownership and exploitation of the Mississippi Valley, from Canada to the Gulf. At the same time, the company took over the collection and administration of taxes. Thus a giant corporation did the business of the state, and to some extent replaced it. An authority, we might call it today.

France bubbled with joy and confidence. The old vexatious system of tax farming—by which the right to collect taxes was sold to the highest bidder, who would then mercilessly persecute the taxpayers—was abolished, and most of the tax collectors discharged. Law planned to substitute a single tax on land for the whole clumsy tax structure. He remitted fifty-two million francs in taxes and annulled internal customs duties on food and fuel. He undertook social services, building hospitals and de-creeing free tuition at the University of Paris. He proposed to seize the immense properties of the church and distribute them to the poor.

To Americans, a fascinating feature of the System is the colonization of the Mississippi basin. Emigrants were lured by tales of mountains filled with gold, silver, and even emeralds, which could be had from the welcoming natives in exchange for knives, saucepans, looking glasses, or flasks of brandy. (A returning official named Cadillac denounced this publicity as humbug. He was promptly jailed; but Fame has made him ample amends.) When volunteers hung back, vagabonds and prostitutes were shipped out from the Paris prisons. Law's agents founded New Orleans, named for the regent; and had the System endured, Law might have created a New France, joined to Canada, strong enough to bar the advance of the English colonists beyond the Appalachians.

In Paris, speculation in company shares rose to a frenzy. Money was lent by the half-hour at high rates; fortunes were made during *le déjeuner.* By December, 1719, shares were selling at forty times their face value. The circulation of bank notes rose to well over two billion francs. The noblest fought for Law's attention. One great lady had her coach wrecked at his door to draw him to the window. His son played with the young king; his eight-year-old daughter gave a ball attended by the highest nobility and the papal nuncio.

In the spring of 1720 Law, who was now *contrôleur-général des finances* of France, tried to apply deflationary pressures, but it was too late. The noble insiders cashed in, carrying off cartloads of gold. The outsiders followed; the buying frenzy was succeeded by a selling frenzy. The regent turned against Law and undermined confidence in the paper currency. On November 1 paper money was outlawed. There were many suicides of paper millionaires who hadn't a penny to buy food. "The Mississippi" became "the Mississippi Bubble."

The end came soon. In December Law fled with his young son to Brussels. He carried with him only sixteen hundred francs and a handsome diamond. He had spent all his vast wealth in the service of his ideas, disdaining to deposit gold outside France. Lady Catherine remained in Paris by choice; the two never met again.

Law was still a notable figure in the great world. The czar invited him to Russia to advise on state finances, but he demurred. He traveled from Copenhagen to London on the English admiral's flagship (in October, 1721). King George I received him cordially and quashed the thirty-year-old condemnation for murder. Law drifted, finally, to Venice, where Montesquieu interviewed him and reported that he was "more in love with his ideas than with money."

At nightfall he would appear in the sumptuous Ridotto, in each of whose leather-lined halls sat a wigged and gowned nobleman holding the bank. Law, reversing the role of his great days, played against the bank. He still had his great diamond, which he left frequently in pawn. His last sitting in the Ridotto, on February 25, 1729, was triumphant: he won enough to pay his debts and redeem his diamond. He left the halls in a fever and took to his bed. The French ambassador visited him—not so much out of sympathy as to scout, in vain, for hidden wealth. He died on March 21, almost fifty-nine.

Lady Catherine lived on. Voltaire saw her in Brussels, destitute. She died in 1747. Her son by John Law joined the Austrian army and died of smallpox.

In lieu of progeny John Law left behind him a remarkable record of achievement. He defined the modern concept of a bank, with its employment of credit, its free circulation of checks, and its bank notes as legal tender under state supervision. He recognized the essential nature of money. He forecast many modern politico-economic theories, including the managed economy of Keynes and the neo-Keynesians. Specifically, he halved the French debt and permitted the monarchy to stagger on toward the Deluge. His principles encouraged the industrial development of eighteenth-century France. His *Compagnie des Indes* prospered for years after his death. His colony of Louisiana struggled, sickly indeed, toward its great destiny. The Mississippi Bubble exploded in glory.

His errors were many—his failure to provide an industrial basis for profit making, his surrender to inflationary pressures, his restrictive decrees. The gambler in him too often made the financier's decisions.

John Law was more right than wrong. But one might just as well be wrong as be right too soon.

M. Licinius Crassus.
Loser.

This Roman general took fifty thousand disciplined, well-equipped troops, marched them into an Oriental desert, and then made every military mistake possible. The result was unprecedented disaster

By CHARLES FAIR

Marcus Licinius Crassus was a commander, a politician, and a financial virtuoso whose weaknesses, though grave, were anything but idiosyncratic. He was, in a sense, the all-American Roman of his day. De Tocqueville has remarked that "in democracies men are never stationary; a thousand chances waft them to and fro . . . Their life is always the sport unforeseen . . . Thus they are often obliged to do things which they have imperfectly learned, to say things which they imperfectly understand, and to devote themselves to work for which they are unprepared by long apprenticeship."

That was exactly Crassus' situation. The Rome in which he grew up was a disintegrating republic in which men were not wafted but hurled to and fro, many thousands being killed in the process. On the whole he met the challenge of his age with phenomenal success. But circumstances, added to his intense natural competitiveness, drove him to undertake too much. At the

time, military campaigning was one of the shorter routes to political eminence, and Crassus quite naturally took it. In whatever he did he showed great drive and tenacity and that combination of expansive optimism and devotion to his own purposes that in America is supposed to be unbeatable. His only major reverse was his last. Like the tycoons of the 1920's, Crassus went out big. History took note of him.

The Rome in which he grew up was disintegrating partly, or perhaps chiefly, as the result of a succession of victorious wars overseas. By 100 B.C. (when he was fifteen) the small farmers and landholders of old republican times were gone. Long years of military conscription, added to the pressure of big-city finance, had long since deprived these independent producers of their lands and their very existence as a class. They disappeared into the mass of urban poor, and the farms they had owned were consolidated into huge estates and worked by slaves.

The Roman world of this era was dominated by an increasingly unbridled realism, which showed itself not merely in the Romans' popular entertainments and their expansionism abroad but also in their politics. Just before Crassus was born, attempts at reform, under the Gracchi, had been bloodily suppressed. And with that, it appears, the attitude of both major parties—the oligarchs, or effective patriciate, represented by the Senate, and the *proletarii,* represented by the Popular Assembly —hardened to the point that neither would stop at anything.

The result, in Crassus' lifetime, was civil war, which first went in favor of the proletarians, under Marius and Cinna, and then in favor of the oligarchs, under Sulla. In savagery these wars had no parallel in the history of the republic, and with them the last remnants of Roman character seem to have been destroyed. After the victory of Sulla, in 82 B.C., the republic was dead in the sense that few still accepted

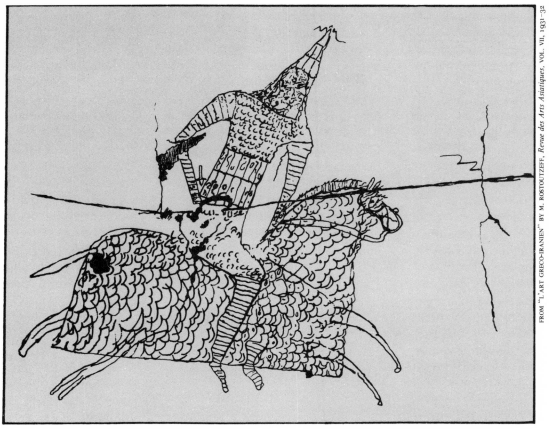

FROM "L'ART GRECO-IRANIEN" BY M. ROSTOUTZEFF, *Revue des Arts Asiatiques*, VOL. VII, 1931–32

In 53 B.C. Roman infantrymen first encountered heavily mailed Parthian lancers like the one shown in this graffito, done in Dura Europos, Syria, many years after the Romans, led by Crassus, were defeated.

the principles of mutual respect, compromise, and regard for law upon which its existence had depended.

Men now failed to honor those obligations of class and country that common sense should have told them were important to their own survival, let alone to the continuance of a civilized or even tolerable society. Life became a struggle for personal eminence, in which one's only loyalty was to the success of the leader for as long as it might last. As a leader, one's only loyalty was to oneself. Unable to bear the strain of events that cost them so much and repaid them so little, large numbers of the commonalty retreated into a violent, almost demented, religiousness. At higher social levels, institutions could no longer enlist that dedication to ideals that might have enabled them to withstand the brilliant adventurers who made the republic their natural prey and eventually their private property.

At the start of the revolutionary epoch—in the days of the Gracchi—the issue had been clear enough. Unless certain concessions were made to the deprived majority, the electoral process would soon become meaningless and the republic itself would fail. Whether or not the form of the state was changed, the apathy of its citizens would guarantee the return of a primitive *Realpolitik*. In fact, that is what occurred. Even as the rapacity of those in power increased, the ordinary voter, instead of seeing the franchise as his last recourse, either ceased to use it or put it up for sale. Meanwhile, Roman power abroad continued to grow without the majority at home clearly consenting to those distant enterprises or really understanding them.

In this tumultuous age Crassus arose. He came of the equestrian order, roughly equivalent to the industrial peerage of England or the upper middle class in America. His name has the same Latin root as our word "crass" (*crassus,* meaning "fat, gross, dense").

He always had a keen sense not only of the odds—he allied himself with Sulla against the popular party—but also of the ways in which national disaster could be turned to private account.

He began his military career in 84 B.C. with the sack of the town of Malaca (Málaga) in Spain. With some of his campaign expenses thus paid in advance, he proceeded to North Africa and thence to Italy, where he became one of Sulla's commanders—according to Plutarch a fairly good one. During this period he grew immensely rich, chiefly, it appears, by buying up at a discount the property of various citizens proscribed by his leader. In the same period he came into rivalry with the young Pompey, whom Sulla rated very high among his field officers.

Plutarch relates that "Pompey was the younger man and his father had had a bad reputation in Rome . . . yet . . . Pompey stood out as conspicuously great, so much so that Sulla treated him with a respect that he seldom showed even to older men . . . he would rise at his approach and uncover his head, and he saluted him by the name of 'Imperator.' All this had a most mortifying effect on Crassus and made him jealous, though in fact Sulla had excellent reasons for preferring Pompey to him, since Crassus was lacking in experience and allowed the lustre of his achievements to be tarnished by his two innate vices of avarice and meanness."*

This jealousy of Pompey was eventually to be the undoing of Crassus. Plutarch makes much of Crassus' greed, but in his fervor as a moralist, may have misunderstood his man. There can be no doubt that Crassus had an eye for a deal, but if avarice was really his ruling passion, it is hard to explain why he continued in politics and the army long after he had become probably the richest man in Rome. Why didn't he retire, like Sulla, or simply go on making money in civilian life? The answer, I think, may be that Crassus was less a financial genius than a competitor par excellence. In forcing his way to the top he used the likeliest means that presented themselves, of which money was one.

Crassus' greatest military success, as well as the critical point in his personal development, came during his campaign against Spartacus. The Spartacan revolt, which began as a minor disturbance nearly a decade after the close of the civil wars, turned into a national calamity overnight. It started in 73 B.C., when a handful of gladiators armed with kitchen knives and spits fought their way out of Capua and seized some wagonloads of arms on the highroad. They won several pitched battles and quickly grew to an army of ninety thousand. Spartacus soundly defeated the praetor Varinus at Lucania, and moving northward in the following year, did the same to every Roman commander sent against him. He apparently planned to fight his way out of the Italian peninsula and then disband his men and permit them to return to their homelands.

*Translated by Rex Warner, Penguin Books

He was well on his way to success when the Senate, in some alarm (and possibly at the prompting of certain privately interested parties), gave Crassus the command against him. In their first engagement Spartacus repulsed, with heavy losses, two legions, under Crassus' lieutenant, Mummius. Sensing the gravity of the situation, Crassus severely punished the survivors, requiring soldiers who had abandoned gear to replace it at their own expense and decimating a cohort (about six hundred men) that had led the rout.

"Crassus decided to settle the Parthian question; the politics of the day required no Tonkin Gulf incident to permit him to do so."

He next maneuvered Spartacus into the peninsula of Rhegium and tried to bottle him up by digging an enormous ditch across the isthmus. But Spartacus broke out of this trap, says Plutarch, waiting for "a night when it was snowing and a wintry storm had got up" and extricating a third of his army by means of bridges of boughs and earth. His troops, however, sensed a turn in their fortunes and became mutinous. During the disorder Crassus surprised a detachment of Spartacans encamped near Lake Lucania, falling upon them in force and inflicting severe casualties. Although Spartacus himself arrived in time to prevent a massacre, Crassus now had the measure of his opponent and apparently felt that decisive victory was within his reach. According to Plutarch, he "regretted that he had previously written to the senate to ask them to send for Lucullus from Thrace and Pompey from Spain. He made all the haste he could to finish the war before these generals arrived."

In a surprise attack that miscarried at the last minute, Crassus managed to kill 12,300 of the enemy and force Spartacus to retreat into the mountains. Though Spartacus was able to rout his pursuers, his success was his undoing: the slaves, now elated and overconfident, forced him to seek a decisive engagement with Crassus—as Plutarch says, "precisely what Crassus most wanted them to do." Spartacus marched back into Lucania and fought a pitched battle in which his army was destroyed and "he himself, surrounded by enemies, still stood his ground and died fighting to the last."

At this point Pompey arrived to take part in the mopping-up operations and—unfortunately for Crassus—to claim most of the credit for suppressing the slave rebellion. He was honored with a triumph in the capital, while Crassus had to settle for a mere ovation. This turn of events may have ruined Crassus by inflaming wild ambitions he should never have had in the first place. For in an age that was coming to respect force before all else, he had the extreme bad luck to have as his companions in power the two best military brains of the day. The top of the pecking order was denied him.

Moreover, he was getting on in years, well into that period of life when the character of a man may set in strange shapes. Plutarch reports a change of this kind in Crassus, in whom "a new passion, in addition to his old weakness of avarice, began to show itself. The glorious exploits of Caesar made Crassus also long for trophies and triumphs—the one field of activity in which he was not, he considered, Caesar's superior. This passion of his gave him no rest . . ."

His chance came after he and Pompey had frustrated, by violence, a last attempt at a consular election, and after the triumvirs, having secured their own consulships by proclamation, had parceled up the Roman world between them. Caesar, to the distress of future schoolboys, already held Gaul. Pompey drew Spain, and Crassus Syria.

Roman influence in the Middle East reached only as far as the Euphrates.

Beyond, in Mesopotamia and Persia, lay the feudal kingdom of the Parthians. Besides being a tricky and elusive foe, the Parthians had for a time been taking turns with Rome in making a "client" state of Armenia. They were thus not only beyond Roman power but powerful enough themselves to be a perennial threat and a nuisance. Crassus decided to settle the Parthian question; the politics of the day required no Tonkin Gulf incident to permit him to do so. He was at this time about sixty, says Plutarch, and "showed by his evident delight that he regarded this as the best piece of good fortune that had ever come to him." Once the idea of suppressing the Parthians had taken hold of him, it led to still grander projects. He dreamed of Eastern conquests like those of Alexander the Great.

Crassus' expedition began badly enough. Accustomed as the Romans were to war, the sheer arbitrariness of this one, which Crassus himself had perhaps made all too plain, aroused public resistance. Ateius, a tribune of the people, attempted to block his departure, and Crassus was obliged —with what feelings one can imagine —to ask Pompey for help. As soon as the people saw Pompey "with a bright and cheerful face," says Plutarch, "they calmed down and stood aside in silence..." Ateius thereupon had Crassus forcibly detained, but as the other tribunes could not agree on the matter, Crassus was released, Ateius calling down on him "curses which were dreadful and frightening enough in themselves and made still more dreadful by the names of certain strange and terrible deities..." As one of the last of the old Romans—that is, a public-spirited citizen and man of conscience —Ateius had risked his neck to keep Crassus from what he regarded as an immoral folly. But too much power had already passed into the hands of the new men.

Following the contretemps with Ateius, Crassus proceeded to the port of Brundisium, where he was in such haste to set sail that he put to sea in a storm and lost a number of ships. The Roman commander in Syria at the time of his arrival was Gabinius, who had been campaigning with some success against the Parthians. Crassus relieved him, and during the summer of 54 B.C. prepared his own offensive. He was convinced that instead of taking the round-about route through Armenia, he should advance directly across the Mesopotamian desert and count on the support of various towns in the region that had long been under Parthian control.

At this stage Crassus made several bad mistakes. The worst in Plutarch's view was his failure to occupy Babylon and Seleucia to the south—cities that "had always been hostile to the Parthians..." Instead, "he was working out what revenues could be drawn from the various cities; many days were spent over scales and balances while he weighed the treasures of the goddess at Hierapolis..." To be fair, however, taking those two distant cities might well have cost more than they were really worth.

"Accustomed as the Romans were to war, the sheer arbitrariness of this one ... aroused public resistance."

More serious, however, was Crassus' failure to acquaint himself with his enemy. He had at least two sources of information—Gabinius, the experienced commander, and the Roman soldiers from Mesopotamian garrisons who had seen "what methods of warfare they employed . . ." The Parthians concentrated on cavalry, using mounted archers and lancers. Plutarch gives the soldiers' report: " 'These people,' they said 'are impossible to shake off if they are in pursuit, and impossible to overtake if they are in flight; they employ a new kind of missile which travels faster than sight and pierces through whatever is in the way . . .' "

By combining exceptional firepower and mobility, the Parthians had developed a hit-and-run, Panzer type of warfare that was quite modern in concept. What they seem to have lacked was the infantry and the staying power for stand-up combat, with the result that they won few decisive victories against the Romans but fought many successful rearguard actions. In this sense they were a guerrilla force, like the modern Viet Cong. Crassus' problem, like General Westmoreland's, was somehow to pin them down—to trap them into fighting on disadvantageous terrain. There is no sign that Crassus understood the situation. He must have thought that a conventional Roman search-and-destroy operation would do the trick.

His next mistake was to refuse the advice of King Artavasdes of Armenia, who came to his camp with six thousand troops, and, in the words of Plutarch, "urged Crassus to invade Parthia by way of Armenia, pointing out that, if he did so, he would not only be leading his army through country which was well supplied (the king himself would see to that), but would also be marching in safety, since the Parthians' one strong point was their cavalry and here Crassus would have the protection of mountains, continuous lines of hills, and country generally unsuited for cavalry operations." Crassus, "without showing any enthusiasm," refused. If this report is true, Crassus must have had little grasp of the tactical difficulties he would face on the sandy plains of Mesopotamia.

He made his final mistake on the field. Having taken his army out of winter quarters in 53 B.C., he proceeded to Zeugma (northwest of Antioch) and there crossed the Euphrates. His force consisted of seven legions (approximately forty-two thousand men), four thousand cavalry, and an equal number of light infantry. At this point his aide Cassius advised him either to make for some fortified Roman town, from which he could safely reconnoiter, or to proceed northward along the riverbank toward Seleucia, thus keeping his right flank covered and guaranteeing a line of supply by water. Crassus did neither. Instead, he took the advice of a local Arab chief named Ariamnes, who claimed that only a token force of Parthians, under Surena, opposed the Romans, while the Parthian king, Hyrodes, was hanging back, reluctant to risk a real war. The Arab urged Crassus to attack Surena at once, before the king decided to commit his main forces.

Perhaps inflamed by the idea of a quick victory, and entirely indifferent to the difficulty of forcing a mobile enemy to stand and fight in open country, Crassus not only trusted the Arab's word but engaged him as a guide. After the Romans had gone some distance into the desert, Artavasdes, back in Armenia, sent word that he had been attacked by Hyrodes and therefore could not provide any reinforcements for Crassus. He suggested that Crassus turn back and join forces with him against Hyrodes and again warned him against an encounter in the open with the Parthians. Tactless as ever, Crassus declined to join forces and added that he would "make Artavasdes pay for his treachery." Having thus cost himself an ally, Crassus now lost his Arab guide, who abruptly departed. The Roman army, numbering close to fifty thousand men, was left stranded in the Mesopotamian desert somewhere east of the Euphrates, not far from the river Belias and the fortified town of Carrhae (Haran).

Shortly afterward, as the army was moving east toward the Belias, scouts reported that the enemy was at hand. Thunderstruck, Crassus began to organize and reorganize his battle order; he then marched on to the river, where his thirsty troops refreshed themselves. Now, something of his old aggressiveness must have returned. At the prompting of his son Publius Crassus,

he decided to seek an engagement at once; he ordered his men to eat in ranks and pressed on at quick march.

When the Parthian army first came into view, it appeared to be no very great force. Their leader, Surena, says Plutarch, "had hidden his main force behind the front ranks and had ordered them to cover themselves with coats and skins so as to conceal the glittering of their armour." Surena had also made certain other preparations—one being to dispense with infantry for this engagement, the other to back up his ten thousand mounted archers with a thousand supply camels. The first move increased his mobility, the second his firepower. This reserve of firepower may be what upset Crassus' calculations. Like other Roman commanders before him in the Eastern theater, he

---

"The disaster at Carrhae
was a severe blow
to Roman military prestige.
To their credit,
however, the Romans knew
a morass when
they saw one and seldom
thereafter
ventured into Parthia."

---

seems to have counted on withstanding a concentrated but necessarily brief barrage from the enemy's archers, after which he could close with the main body in the conventional manner. But Surena had misled Crassus about his plans and numbers. He maneuvered the Romans onto a battleground of his own choosing, anticipated their moves, and finally, just before he struck, made skillful use of psychological shock-tactics.

After showing the enemy an apparently small, unarmored cavalry detachment, he quickly deployed his forces in full battle array and ordered them to sound the drums. ". . . first of

all the whole plain was filled with a deep and terrifying roaring sound. . . . Before the Romans had recovered from their consternation at this din, the enemy suddenly dropped the coverings of their armour. Now they could be seen clearly, their helmets and breastplates blazing like fire, their Margianian steel glittering keen and bright, their horses armoured with plates of bronze and steel."

The Romans meantime formed into a square. The mounted Parthian lancers tried to break this line, but seeing the depth and density of the infantry formations they decided to give "the impression that they were breaking their ranks and losing all cohesion"; instead they encircled the unwary Romans. They now released a terrible rain of arrows on Crassus' troops, driving back his skirmishers and inflicting startling casualties in the main body, by virtue of "how strong and fast these Parthian arrows were . . . The Parthians now spread out and began to shoot their arrows from all sides at once. There was no attempt at accurate marksmanship, since the Romans were so densely crowded together that it was impossible to miss the target even if one wished to do so." When the Romans tried to counterattack, the Parthians, being mounted, easily drew out of reach, firing as they went—an art in which, Plutarch says, only the Scythians were their superiors; "and it is certainly a very clever manoeuvre—to fight and to look after one's own safety at the same time, so that there is no dishonour in running away." A modern writer would see this simply as a superior tactic, the sort of thing armored formations do when forced to retire.

As the archery barrage continued, Crassus "saw no end to it all" and ordered his son Publius to mount a more determined counterattack. Publius, with a force of thirteen hundred horse, five hundred archers, and eight cohorts of heavy infantry, set out to charge the Parthians, who fled before them. Encouraged, Publius sent the cavalry in pursuit, he himself following with his foot soldiers. The object of the Parthian withdrawal was soon clear enough, for when Publius and his men had gone some distance, the enemy suddenly reappeared in force; but instead of attacking frontally, they rode round and round the legionaries.

Plutarch says that they raised "great masses of sand which fell from the air in a continual shower so that the Romans could scarcely see or speak. Huddled together in a narrow space and getting into each other's way, they were shot down by the arrows. Nor did death come to them either easily or quickly. . . . They would writhe as the arrows struck them; they would break them off in their wounds and then lacerate and disfigure their own bodies by trying to tear out by main force the barbed arrow heads . . . When Publius called on them to attack the enemy's armoured cavalry, they showed him hands pinioned to their shields, feet nailed through into the ground . . . Publius therefore urged on his cavalry, charged forward with them boldly," and though having the worst of it in some ways, did better in others. His mounted Gauls carried lances too light to be effective against the heavily armored Parthians, so they switched to the tactic of seizing the enemy's lance and wrestling him to the ground, where his armor made him nearly helpless. Alternatively, the Gauls leapt from their horses and disemboweled the enemy's mounts, unseating riders and causing general confusion.

But the Romans were greatly outnumbered and had already sustained losses too severe to have any hope of winning. Publius retreated to a nearby hill with the remnants of his force, and there he fought on to the end, ordering his armor-bearer to run him through when his wounds had incapacitated him. Two of his aides likewise took their own lives, and all but five hundred out of a force of approximately six and a half thousand died fighting.

With this disaster, the battle of Carrhae was really over, although Crassus was not yet aware of it. When news of the Romans' desperate position finally got through, Crassus was apparently stunned. By the time he began to move, he found the entire enemy force converging upon him once again. With this advancing host rode a Parthian trooper carrying the head of Publius on his lance for all the legionaries to see. Crassus rallied bravely, but the morale of his men was broken. Having no recourse, they fought on, with great losses, until nightfall.

"Rome simply could not afford Crassus, who paid what some might consider a fair price for the suffering and disaster he brought upon others."

During the night they managed a disorderly retreat to Carrhae—a move made terrible by the cries of the wounded left behind, some four thousand of whom the Parthians slaughtered the next morning. Crassus' problem now, of course, was to extricate himself from a siege. Incredibly, he entertained the hope that the Armenians would come to his rescue. He repeated his earlier mistake of hiring a guide—this time a spy named Andromachus, who promised to lead him from Carrhae by night. What was left of the Roman expeditionary force would break up and go its several ways under various commanders, some of whom did in fact escape.

But Surena was determined that Crassus should not elude him; Andromachus was a decoy sent to lead Crassus into a trap. Once attacked, however, Crassus' pathetic force managed to rally and defend him. Surena, again trading on Crassus' credulity, persuaded him that he meant to sign an honorable peace and lured him into the Parthian camp. There Crassus was killed. Of his army of about fifty thousand, 40 per cent were said to have been killed and an additional 20 per cent taken prisoner.

The disaster at Carrhae was a severe blow to Roman military prestige. To their credit, however, the Romans knew a morass when they saw one and seldom thereafter ventured into Parthia. Had Crassus lived, he might have gone interminably on with his enterprise, like some generals of a later age. As a statesman he foreshadows those of our own time who, having adopted nonsensical policies, refuse under any circumstances to give them up. As a commander he is the prototype of the modern general who hopes to bludgeon his way to victory by sheer technical and numerical superiority. Such a commander counts heavily upon "energy of will" (in the phrase of General Westmoreland), which is to say, less upon intelligence than upon pure resolve backed up by material resources. One goes forth simply as the representative of the better anthill. The difficulty was that Rome was not *that much* better than Parthia; it simply could not afford Crassus, who paid what some might consider a fair price for the suffering and disaster he brought upon others. A loser could expect to be left to his fate, but Western civilization long ago abandoned this elementary system of justice. Nowadays the very worst of commanders is apt to be safe both on the field (it is almost unheard of for a general to be captured in battle) and in his later career. The custom in civilized nations is not to cashier or execute generals for their more ghastly mistakes but to promote them to still higher posts where they can do less harm. In the days of the Roman republic, however, this curious solution to the problem of military incompetence had not yet been devised.

Charles Fair is a neuroscientist and author, whose book on military history—from which this article is taken—will be published this fall by Simon and Schuster, Inc. It is entitled From the Jaws of Victory, *and it is a chronicle of "the consequences of stupidity in high places."*

How to Choose a Royal Bride

From Henry VII to Prince Charles: here are twenty-four male chauvinist questions to ask of any prospect

Prince Charles may already have given the matter some thought; certainly it has not escaped the protocol people at Buckingham Palace (to say nothing of his parents) that one of these days he will be expected to choose a bride. Fleet Street, home of some of the world's most imaginative journalists, has lately begun trying his crown for size on a succession of English celebrities, notably Arabella Churchill—a symbolic match, like the marriage of the doge to the sea, that would probably break all popularity records.

It would come as no surprise if Charles does decide to marry some swinging English girl, for it has become fairly well established that royalty are free to marry whom they please. No one demonstrated this more decisively than Princess Margaret when she opted for a photographer, and most of the people in her peer group have recently seen fit to follow her example: the Crown Prince of Norway is married to a commoner, the Crown Princess of the Netherlands to an untitled German diplomat, and the Crown Princess of Denmark to a French count of very modest lineage.

But Charles, despite his proven abilities as a crowd-pleaser, is inclined to be a traditionalist, and there is a good chance that he will revert to the ancient precedent holding that the sons of rulers should marry the daughters of rulers. In times past this sometimes brought significant gains in territory and prestige: Scotland became British by marriage, for example, just as Castile and Aragon became Spanish by marriage.

Today, no one whom Charles can marry can add an inch of territory to his domain, but if she is a real princess, as opposed to a debutante or a film star, she will be far better equipped to face the trial-by-publicity that awaits the next Queen of England, not just during the wedding, but for the rest of her life. In that lonely, taxing role only a real princess will be above reproach. It will be an advantage if she looks good on television, can generate enthusiasm in Melbourne, Colombo, and Saskatchewan, and can satisfy the mother-yearnings of the nation. But whatever her shortcomings (and no matter who she is, it may be impossible to pretend, as the English do about Elizabeth II, that she has none), it will always be remembered that she is a real princess and entitled to her coronet.

If Charles does decide to pick a bride from the remaining royal houses of Europe, he will find his choice rather limited. The ruling houses of Scandinavia, Holland, and Greece, with whom the Windsors have close family ties, have no unmarried princesses who are younger than the twenty-two-year-old Charles. An older wife is presumably out of the running. Since Henry VIII's ill-starred marriage to his brother's widow, Catherine of Aragon, only two queens of England have been older than their husbands, and both by just a few months: Queen Victoria was three months older than Prince Albert, and Queen Caroline six months older than King George II.

The list of possible princesses is headed by two Belgians: Princess Marie Christine, twenty, and Princess Marie Esmeralda, fifteen, both daughters of ex-King Leopold III and his second wife, Princess Liliane (who was born a commoner). Dynastically far more eligible, however, is Leopold's granddaughter in neighboring Luxembourg, seventeen-year-old Princess Marie-Astrid, whose background is impeccably royal on both sides. Her mother, born Princess Josephine Charlotte of Belgium, was the only daughter of the popular Queen Astrid, and her father, Grand Duke Jean, is the son of Grand Duchess Charlotte and Prince Felix of Bourbon-Parma. If Charles were to marry Marie-Astrid, she would become the first Bourbon princess to sit on the British throne since Charles I married Henrietta Maria in 1625.

Charles's matrimonial choice would become much wider if he considered princesses from families who have lost their thrones. In Germany there are at least four unmarried Hohenzollern princesses, descendants of both the Kaiser and Queen Victoria, as well as three princesses of Saxe-Coburg-Gotha (Prince Albert's house), two of Saxe-Weimar, and a dozen others of such dimly remembered states as Hanover, Lippe, and Mecklenburg.

The five daughters of ex-King Michael of Rumania—including Margarita, twenty-two, Elena, twenty, and Irina, eighteen—are all, like Charles, descendants of Queen Victoria. So is the seventeen-year-old Grand Duchess Marie of Russia, who lives in Madrid, and the two English-born princesses of Prussia, Victoria, nineteen, and Antonia, sixteen.

If these ex-royal princesses are taken into account, there is certainly no lack of young ladies who could be considered genealogically qualified to become Queen of England. Before Charles makes a move in any direction, however, his matrimonial intelligence staff will want to know a great deal more about each prospect. A future king must be even more careful than an ordinary man when it comes to selecting a wife. Questionnaires will have to be prepared, background reports submitted, emissaries discreetly dispatched. In such delicate affairs of state, as in all matters touching upon the royal prerogative, it is advisable to rely on precedent and tradition.

Fortunately, there are certain historical guidelines that Charles and his advisors can consult when they sit down to decide precisely what a king ought to know about a prospective bride. An earlier incumbent, Henry VII of England, prepared just such a questionnaire when he set out to acquire a second queen in 1505, and his questions are so acutely relevant that they could serve as the basis for any similar search today.

As a marriage expert, Henry VII's reputation has been eclipsed by that of his son Henry VIII, but during his lifetime he was highly regarded as a judge of both women and horses. In 1505, after the death of his queen (of natural causes), Ferdinand and Isabella of Spain proposed that he marry their niece, the recently widowed Queen Juana of Naples, who was then living in Valencia with her mother, the old Queen. Though Henry was fifty-one to Juana's twenty-seven, he was not unwilling to consider the idea. Three envoys—Francis Marsyn, James Braybrooke, and John Stile—were sent to Spain to report in detail on the lady's potentialities.

Henry himself drew up the long list of questions cataloguing everything he wanted to know about the young queen, together with instructions to have her portrait painted as naturalistically as possible. Sir Francis Bacon called his questions "curious and exquisite," and thought they indicated that Henry was very chaste, "for that he meant to find all Things in one Woman, and so to settle his affections

without ranging." Whatever the motive may have been, there has rarely been a more candid statement of the things that really matter to a man about a woman. Here is the substance of his questions, translated from the Tudor into modern English and slightly condensed, together with the gist of his ambassadors' replies:

ITEM 1: Mark the state that the two Queens keep . . .

ANSWER: They do keep a great household of gentlemen, ladies, gentlewomen and slaves, and the old Queen keeps a great estate and with great gravity, for she has the King's full power to rule all the realm of Valencia.

ITEM 2: Mark how they be accompanied and what lords and ladies they have about them.

ANSWER: We saw great suits and many suitors come before the old Queen. . . .

ITEM 3: Mark the young Queen's discretion, wisdom and gravity.

ANSWER: The young Queen with a sad and noble countenance uttered such words as pleased her . . . after the manner of that country with a noble gravity and not too bold, but somewhat shamefaced womanly.

ITEM 4: Learn whether the young Queen speaks any other languages than

Spanish and Italian, and whether she can speak any French or Latin.

ANSWER: The young Queen can speak no languages except Spanish and Italian; it is said that she understands both Latin and French, but she speaks none.

ITEM 5: Specially mark and note well the age and stature of the said young Queen and the features of her body.

ANSWER: She is twenty-seven years old and not much more; as to the stature of her person we cannot know perfectly, for when we came unto her presence Her Grace was sitting on a pillow. . . . Her Grace ever had on her a great mantilla (after the manner of that country), so that a man shall not lightly perceive anything but the visage.

ITEM 6: Mark the favor of her visage, whether she be painted or not and whether it be fat or lean, sharp or round, and whether her countenance is cheerful and amiable, frowning or melancholy, steadfast or light or blushing in communication.

ANSWER: The Queen is not painted and the favor of her visage is of a very good compass and amiable and somewhat round and fat; the countenance cheerful and not frowning and steadfast, not light or boldhardly, in speech, but with a demure, womanly shamefaced countenance . . .

ITEM 7: Note the clearness of her skin.

ANSWER: The Queen is very fair and clear of skin, as far as we could perceive by her face, neck and hands.

ITEM 8: Note the color of her hair.

ANSWER: It would seem her hair is brown.

ITEM 9: Note well her eyes, brows, teeth and lips.

ANSWER: The Queen's eyes be of color brown but somewhat grayish; her brows brown and very small, like a wire of hair; her teeth fair and clean, and as far as we could perceive, well set. Her lips are somewhat round and thick, which right well becomes the said Queen.

ITEM 10: Mark well the fashion of her nose, and the height and breadth of her forehead.

By FREDERIC V. GRUNFELD

ANSWER: The fashion of her nose is a little rising in the midward and a little bowing towards the end, and she is much like nosed unto the Queen her mother. As to her forehead, we could not perfectly discern its height or breadth because in that country they wear their kerchiefs down to their brows.

ITEM 11: Note her complexion.

ANSWER: The Queen is of a very fair, sanguine complexion and clean.

ITEM 12: Mark her arms whether they be great or small, long or short.

ANSWER: Her arms be somewhat round and not very small, so far as we could perceive when she put forth her hand when we kissed it; the length of her arm is of a good proportion . . .

ITEM 13: See whether her hands be fat or lean . . .

ANSWER: Three sundry times we kissed her said hands, noting the Queen to be right fair-handed; they be somewhat fully and soft and fair and clean skinned.

ITEM 14: Note her fingers whether they be long or short, small or great, broad or narrow.

ANSWER: Her fingers be right fair and small and of a meetly length and breadth.

ITEM 15: Mark whether her neck be long or short, small or great.

ANSWER: The Queen's neck is comely and not mis-shapen, neither very short nor very long.

ITEM 16: Mark her breasts and paps whether they be big or small.

ANSWER: The Queen's breasts be somewhat great and full; they were trussed and somewhat high after the manner of the country, which causes Her Grace to seem much the fuller and her neck to be the shorter.

ITEM 17: Mark whether there be any hair about her lips or not.

ANSWER: As far as we can perceive she has no hair appearing about her lips or mouth, but is very clear skinned.

ITEM 18: Speak with the said young Queen and approach near to her mouth to feel the condition of her breath, whether it be sweet or not.

ANSWER: Her mouth is like for to be of a sweet flavor and well aired.

ITEM 19: Note the fashion of her foot . . .

ANSWER: Her foot is but small, but by the slipper the greatness of her foot cannot be known . . .

ITEM 20: Inquire whether she has commonly been in health or sometime sick.

ANSWER: One Pascarell, a Neapolitan wise man and potecary to the Queens, said that she has been in as much health as any gentlewoman he ever had known.

ITEM 21: Whether she be in any singular favor with the King of Aragon, her uncle, and whether she have any resemblance to him.

ANSWER: The King of Aragon right much loves and favors the young Queen

his niece and intends to promote her unto some excellent marriage . . . She is like unto the King her uncle and specially in the fashion of her nose and complexion.

ITEM 22: Inquire of the manner of her diet and whether she be a great feeder or drinker.

ANSWER: The Queen is a good feeder and eats well her meat twice on a day, but does not drink often and then most commonly water.

ITEM 23: Inquire for some cunning painter, so that he may draw a picture of the visage and semblance of the young Queen. [The portrait, if it ever existed, has not survived.]

ITEM 24: Inquire what land or livelihood the young Queen has, or shall have after the decease of her mother.

ANSWER: The King of Castile gives unto the said Queens fifteen or sixteen thousand ducats yearly out of his coffers for their expenses and maintaining of their estates.

Henry's list would seem to prove that he was a gentleman. Despite his reputation for avarice, nearly all his questions deal with Juana's physical attributes, and only one with her dowry. But the answer to the last question apparently had a discouraging effect. "Alas, it was not by a short neck that the lady lost the day," wrote the historian Martin Hamlyn. "It was her jointure that the wily king thought not big enough for pleasureable handling." At least this is no longer an overweening consideration for an English king, even if Prince Philip has reason to complain about the shrinking value of the royal household money. At Buckingham Palace, one would like to think, two can live as cheaply as one.

Frederic V. Grunfeld, an American, is former editor of the British magazine Queen. *He writes regularly for* HORIZON.

DRAWINGS BY EDWARD SOREL